250N

D0898084

SEMINAR STUDIES IN HISTORY

Editor: Patrick Richardson

RADICAL POLITICS
1790-1900
RELIGION AND UNBELIEF

SEMINAR STUDIES IN HISTORY

Editor: Patrick Richardson

A full list of titles in this
series will be found on the
back cover of this book

SEMINAR STUDIES IN HISTORY

RADICAL POLITICS
1790–1900
RELIGION AND UNBELIEF

Edward Royle

Selwyn College, Cambridge

LONGMAN

LONGMAN GROUP LIMITED
London

ASSOCIATED COMPANIES, BRANCHES AND
REPRESENTATIVES THROUGHOUT THE WORLD

© Longman Group Ltd 1971

First published 1971

ISBN 0 582 31425 9

PRINTED IN GREAT BRITAIN BY
WESTERN PRINTING SERVICES LTD, BRISTOL

Contents

Introduction to the Series

The seminar method of teaching is being used increasingly in VI forms and at universities. It is a way of learning in smaller groups through discussion, designed both to get away from and to supplement the basic lecture techniques. To be successful, the members of a seminar must be informed, or else—in the unkind phrase of a cynic—it can be a 'pooling of ignorance'. The chapter in the textbook of English or European history by its nature cannot provide material in this depth, but at the same time the full academic work may be too long and perhaps too advanced for students at this level.

For this reason we have invited practising teachers in universities, schools and colleges of further education to contribute short studies on specialised aspects of British and European history with these special needs and pupils of this age in mind. For this series the authors have been asked to provide, in addition to their basic analysis, a full selection of documentary material of all kinds and an up-to-date and comprehensive bibliography. Both these sections are referred to in the text, but it is hoped that they will prove to be valuable teaching and learning aids in themselves.

Note on the System of References:

A bold number in round brackets (**5**) in the text refers the reader to the corresponding entry in the Bibliography section at the end of the book.

A bold number in square brackets, preceded by 'doc.' [**docs 6, 8**] refers the reader to the corresponding items in the section of Documents, which follows the main text.

PATRICK RICHARDSON
General Editor

Acknowledgements

We are indebted to the following for permission to quote from copyright material:

Co-operative Union Ltd. for extracts from the Holyoake Papers.

For permission to use the illustration on the cover we are grateful to Cambridge University Library.

I have to thank Dr D. M. Thompson for reading through the typescript of this book, and my wife for her persevering encouragement.

E.R.

Part One

BACKGROUND

1 Religion and the Working Classes

INTRODUCTION

Radical politics in nineteenth-century Britain can be regarded as a series of popular agitations by which an extension of the franchise was won and working-class representation in Parliament made possible. This was the point of view adopted by labour historians of the last generation, who were proud of the traditions and the heritage of the working-class movement in which they took part (**21**), but their approach can now be seen to have had severe limitations. It naturally emphasised those aspects of nineteenth-century radicalism which contributed most to the creation of the modern social democratic state, and neglected other radical ideas and organisations which were equally important at the time, but which now lie among the dead ends of history. The nineteenth-century radicals were not always progressive in their aims, and many of their ideas had more in common with seventeenth- and eighteenth-century concepts than with those of the present day (**25**).

One of the most important changes in British society in the last hundred years has been the decline in the importance of religion. Nineteenth-century radical politics were rooted in religion, but this is not to claim that the modern labour movement has a specifically Christian heritage. The most important element in the making of the working class was certainly not Christian in any orthodox sense: the radical tradition of Thomas Paine was grounded in eighteenth-century deism, and was developed in the nineteenth century by Richard Carlile and the blasphemous and seditious press, by the Socialist followers of Robert Owen, and by the Secularists led by G. J. Holyoake and Charles Bradlaugh.

The development of radical politics between 1790 and 1900 reflects the social, political and intellectual changes which transformed Britain from a predominantly rural and agrarian society into an urban and industrial one. At the end of the eighteenth century, social and economic units were still very small, and society was divided into communities rather than classes. Although attendance at church was not as widespread as has sometimes been assumed, religion was the cement of society, and the Established Church was a powerful support of the aristocratic conservative state. During the nineteenth century, the Churches expanded rapidly, inspired by the Evangelical revival, but the population increased even faster and, as industry spread and towns grew into cities, the institutions of organised religion were unable to maintain their positions in society. The Anglican aristocratic monopoly of power in religious and secular affairs was challenged by the new industrial and commercial middle classes, led in the mid-nineteenth century by men like Richard Cobden and John Bright of the Anti-Corn Law League. The ultra-radical leaders of the lower classes had, for most of the time, to play a secondary rôle and follow the lead of the middle-class parliamentary radicals, but despite this they were able to maintain a distinct tradition throughout the century and gradually developed their own class-consciousness. This they sometimes expressed in economic terms, particularly in the early years of the century when the birth-pangs of industrialisation were felt most by the working classes, but a second distinguishing characteristic of the early radical consciousness was opposition to religion. The ultra-radical leaders were, generally speaking, suspicious of the Christian system which they associated with political oppression, and they were hostile to the Evangelical nonconformity with which the middle classes were identified. Ideas which might today be expressed purely in economic terms were then often given a religious and sectarian form, and the ultra-radical leaders were notoriously 'infidel' or 'atheistic' in their opinions (**60**).

In 1851 a Religious Census was conducted to find out the numerical relationship of the churches to each other and the population as a whole. The growth of the various denominations was carefully narrated and catalogued by Horace Mann (**39**), and the religious population was shown to be almost equally divided between the Established and non-Established churches (**18**). This was upsetting to many Anglicans who feared the figures were inaccurate (**49, 50**), but one conclusion was inescapable and was deplored by all: out of a total of thirteen and a half million people who could have been expected at church on Census Sunday, 30 March 1851, only seven and a quarter million were calculated to have actually attended [**doc. 1**]. From among these 'missing millions' the ultra-radical leaders drew most of their support.

THE FAILURE OF THE CHURCHES

Christian writers in the mid-nineteenth century confirmed Horace Mann's pessimistic picture of the failure of the Churches to reach large numbers of the population, and gave further evidence to his assumption that many of these absentees belonged to the lower orders. The Leicester Unitarian Domestic Missionary reported in 1846 that 'there is an almost universal neglect of public worship in those parts of the town that are occupied by the working classes'. J. W. Hudson, the historian of adult education, wrote in 1851 that 'In one manufactory in Lambeth, where upwards of one thousand men were constantly employed, it was ascertained that no more than thirty-three attended public worship, and only fourteen of them were members of any Christian Church.' The inspector of elementary schools in the Midlands noted in 1846:

> It is stated on good authority that of 5,000 miners of Bilston there are 4,000 who attend no place of worship, and that the whole number of persons arrived at years of discretion in that place and in the district immediately surrounding it who thus entirely neglect the public ordinances of religion, is 11,000 out of a population of 24,000 (**14**).

The Unitarian missionary in Manchester divided the population into four groups: the indifferent, non-professing Christians, members of the various Christian denominations, and unbelievers. The latter two groups he thought to be small. Estimates of their comparative size varied widely. The Reverend J. F. Whitty of St Mary's, Sheffield, told the Evangelical Alliance that 'in his district, which had only a population of 6,000, there were upwards of 1,200 persons who openly avowed atheistical or deistical sentiments', but an Evangelical missionary in Manchester painted an entirely different picture. He told the annual meeting of the City Mission in 1854: 'Besides a good many sceptics, who are practically infidel, I have discovered four or five avowed rejectors of the whole Divine Revelation.' The Unitarian missionary's report agreed that 'infidelity, in the common acceptance of the term, is of very rare occurrence indeed'. The Secularist leader in Birmingham, Christopher Charles Cattell, assumed that very few of the members of his Eclectic Institute would wish to attend his Sunday meetings on religion. 'Young men generally', he said, 'either attend church, or *do not care about religion at all*' [**doc. 4**].

This confusion about the views of the masses who did not attend church arises from attempts at generalisation from limited or local experience. A wide number of views could be held at the same time, and a wide spectrum of opinion and prejudice extends from the man who objected to the local vicar to the man who could give highly philosophical reasons for rejecting the concept of a God. Whatever the articulated views of individuals may have been, the situation described as follows by the Vicar of Leeds in 1846 strikes a note of familiar reality: 'Not one in a hundred attends any place of worship, but the usual practice is for the men to lie in bed on Sunday morning, while the women cook the dinner, and for an adjournment in the evening to take place to a public house.'

Thomas Frost recalled that the inhabitants of Bethnal Green at this time were too preoccupied with the immediate requirements of material existence to have any time for the spiritual (**84**). In this sense the infidel masses were, in the words of the 1851 Census Report, 'unconscious Secularists', but the same people could be very religious, and their opposition to the churches took very specific and irrational forms.

POPULAR PROTEST

The most prevalent form of opposition to religion was anti-clericalism, which was fed as much by Christians as non-Christians. Protestants hated Catholics; Dissenters attacked the Establishment; dissenting Methodists issued fly-sheets about the popery of the clerical Conference. Throughout the nineteenth century, English radicals looked out over a European continent where political reaction ruled supreme in alliance with the clergy of the Catholic Church. Only in Ireland was this not wholly true.

The Church of England was strongly disliked on several grounds. It was hated as the collector of tithes and church rates. Dissenters resented having to pay for parish churches which they seldom used, in addition to their private subscriptions to their own chapels. Edward Miall organised the opposition when, in 1844, he founded the Anti-State Church Association (in 1853 it became the Liberation

Society), and while this organisation existed ammunition was not lacking with which to attack the Establishment. Tithes were a great grievance and of excellent propaganda value, and the church rates could be a serious burden on the poor. Holyoake, the leader of the Secularists, attributed his earliest alienation from the Church to the Easter dues his mother had to pay (**114**). Above all, the Church was hated as the spiritual arm of an oppressive State. At the national level, William Pitt had 'considered the church of England, as by law established, to be so essential a part of the constitution, that whatever endangered it, would necessarily affect the security of the whole' (**12**, 1790). This policy seemed to be confirmed in 1832 when on the first reading of the Reform Bill in the House of Lords, twenty-one bishops voted against, six abstained, and only two voted for. The bishops were probably the most hated of all the clergy. According to a radical Scots Presbyterian, James Murray, whose sermons were reprinted by William Hone in 1819, bishops 'bore as little resemblance to the simple founders of the Christian system, as mountebanks at a country fair to a grave synod of presbyterian elders'. A hostile observer at the end of the eighteenth century, W. H. Reid, reported that anticlericalism was rife among the political societies of the 1790s. A common toast among them was the famous republican sentiment 'May the last King be strangled in the bowels of the last Priest!!!' (**57**) [**doc. 8**].

At the local level, clerical magistrates aroused a deep hatred and contempt. The savage caricatures of the priest in William Hone's *The Political House that Jack Built* and *The Clerical Magistrate* (1819) (*see cover illustration*) were probably inspired by such magistrates as the Reverend Sir B. Dudley of Ely. During the riots in the city in 1816 the other magistrates agreed in Dudley's absence to a two shillings a day increase in wages. Dudley returned, repudiated the agreement, and led the military in an attack on the rioters. For this, the Bishop commended him (**44a**). During the Chartist riots the clergy were not forgotten. In 1842, following Thomas Cooper's speeches in the Potteries, the local miners set fire to the houses of the vicars of Longton and Hanley. This association of the Church with political conservatism was a powerful cause of opposition among the working classes to the institutions of organised religion. The Church seemed to stand in the way of reform, and to be more interested in the next world than in the present one [**doc. 2**].

The Evangelicals with their Bibles were hated almost as much as

7

the priests with their State-dominated Church. This was where the opponents of ecclesiastical Christianity and the Dissenters parted company, for the latter, and particularly the Methodists, were often the worst offenders in the eyes of the radicals. Fantastic claims, spiritual absurdities, and a literal belief in the biblical prophecies so stretched the reason that intelligent men who had been indoctrinated as children often recoiled into infidelity as adults. Joseph Barker, who for a time became a freethinker, described this experience in his own childhood:

> I regarded the contents of the Bible as wholly divine. I believed every word to be true, and every command to be binding, as the law of an almighty and all-perfect God. To doubt the truth or divinity of the Bible, I believed to be the greatest sin of which a man could be guilty. To disbelieve any statement of the Bible, was to call God a liar, and to make sure of eternal damnation. No one could entertain such a doubt, I was assured, but through the suggestion of the devil and none but the most wicked of men would hearken to such suggestions. (*An Answer to the Question How Did You Become An Infidel? . . .*, Holyoake, [1859]).

Such an upbringing was wide open to criticism and doubt, and the discoveries of geology and biology, together with textual criticisms of the Bible, were eagerly seized as a justification for revolt.

The methods of the Evangelicals were also repugnant. Holyoake described revivalism as 'spiritual pocket-picking'—'the Revivalist looks to the end and not the means' (**9**). Arch-Evangelical priests like Hugh Stowell of Salford and Francis Close of Cheltenham were cordially hated. Close banned the local steeplechase, prevented the rebuilding of the theatre, and rejoiced that unbaptised infants were consumed by the fires of hell. Stowell opposed the first government grant to education in 1833, and both men were outspoken critics of Chartism and Socialism (**81**). Despite the many good works of the clergy, these were the actions which helped shape the image of the Churches in the eyes of the working classes. The conservatism of the Anglicans and Wesleyans, the tracts of Hannah More, the probings of the Society for the Suppression of Vice and the legislated dullness of Sundays were largely responsible for the strong antipathy felt by large numbers of the lower classes towards the institutions of religion [**docs 2, 4**].

8

POPULAR CHRISTIANITY

The paradox involved in any description of the masses who did not attend church is that, next to their infidelity, the most common feature about them was their religiosity. The Secularists had no illusions about the appeal of religion to the imagination and feelings of ordinary people. Religion was deeprooted in the community, even in the urban community. The Church provided the folk rites of a timeless way of life. Births, marriages and deaths were occasions when religion made its deepest impact on secular life. The churching of women and confirmation were ancient ceremonies which retained their significance. Harvest festivals and Whit walks were nineteenth-century innovations, but no less influential for that (**55**). Opposition to the Churches led not to atheism but to an attempt to 'purify' the faith and to rediscover 'true' Christianity. Revolt led in the first place to a multitude of Christian sects. Swedenborgians first made their appearance in London in the mid-eighteenth century. By 1851 there were fifty congregations in the country. 'Zion' Ward, a crippled Methodist shoemaker who believed he was the Christ, filled the Blackfriars Rotunda in 1831 with the devoted and the curious, 'Shepherd' Smith preached Pantheism in the 1830s, and Goodwyn Barmby founded the Communist Church in the 1840s. Joseph Barker's followers became the Christian Brethren when he was expelled from the New Connexion in 1841. The Mormons claimed to have converted 50,000 people in the United Kingdom between 1837 and 1850 (**41, 60**). Among the minor sects listed by Mann in the census report were New Christians and Christ's Disciples, Believers and Gospel Refugees, Stephenites and Inghamites, Teetotallers and Israelites (**39**). Popular movements were basically religious and derived much of their power from religion. Richard Oastler, the factory reformer, was a Moravian-trained Wesleyan who had turned Anglican. J. R. Stephens, perhaps the most fiery Chartist of all, was an independent Methodist, who denounced with apocalyptic fervour the sins of the industrial world from his chapel in Ashton. The Primitive Methodists were important in the early development of the trade union movement (**25**). The simple, primitive religion of Christ justified reform in Church and State. William Hone believed one of James Murray's maxims to have been 'that no man could be a real Christian who was not a warm and zealous friend of civil and religious liberty'. Hatred of priests merely confirmed that it was they who were keeping the true Gospel from the people. The Christian idea was more influential than mere church attendance figures suggest. When Samuel Bamford recalled the religious views of his father, he wrote:

> My father . . . was a reader, and amongst the other books which he now read was Paine's *Rights of Man*. He also read Paine's *Age of Reason*, and his other theological works, but they made not the least alteration to his religious opinions. Both he and my uncle had left the society of Methodists, but to the doctrines of John Wesley they continued adherents so long as they lived (**59**).

This kind of religion finds no place in Mann's statistics.

The religious nature of the population is well illustrated by the report which F. Liardet made to the Central Society of Education in 1839 on the 'State of the Peasantry in the County of Kent' [**doc. 3**]. This was an investigation into the background of an anti-Poor Law riot in which men from Herne Hill, Broughton and Dunkirk in Kent had flocked to follow Mad Thoms—*sic*, actually J. N. Tom (**60**)—who claimed to be the reincarnation of Christ. Liardet attributed the incredulity of the people to their exclusively religious education. The only books in the homes were religious—usually the Bible, Prayer Book or a hymn book, rarely all three. The usual decorations in the home, if any, were religious prints. The only subjects taught in school were Bible reading and the Catechism, and this was not untypical of rural England.

Liardet thought that in the crowded towns men would be less subject to superstition than in the countryside, but he did not go so far as to claim that the countryside was Christian and that the towns were not. It does seem, though, that the countryside was generally more favourable to religious influences than the towns, and that the traditional hold of religion might well have been broken when men moved from their small rural communities to the large anonymous towns. The vertically structured society of rural and small town England was weakened or almost totally absent in parts of the new industrial cities. The Reverend Henry Moseley's report on the Midland District schools in 1846 referred to this problem of the poorest, most overcrowded areas in the great towns:

In districts like these, the clergyman occupies a new and an anomalous position. The social edifice in which, in other and more favoured localities, he occupies the most honoured place, stands here in ruins. There is nothing to fill up the space between him and the industrial masses, unless it be the class of small shopkeepers, colliery clerks, and victuallers. It is a desolate position (**14**).

So desolate was it that priests could not be found to go there. Jabez Bunting was reminding the Wesleyan Conference in 1854 that Methodism had principally been a rural system, and their circuits were best adapted to the countryside. Bishop Blomfield could not get good men to minister to his new churches in London. One of the principal contributions of the Oxford Movement to the Anglican Church was that it provided men to work in the slums.

Not all the working-class inhabitants of the towns were slum-dwellers. Those with the leisure and opportunity to read and think had greater scope in the towns for independent thought and activity than their fellows in the countryside. The Bible and the pulpit did not have the time-honoured monopoly of communication. In public houses and coffee shops, on street corners and in back-street halls, in factories and workshops, ideas were developed, hopes shared and plans made. The working-class movements of England were nurtured in the manufacturing towns of the North [**doc. 5**].

THE WORKING CLASSES

Most working-class movements in the nineteenth century were led by men from the élite of the working classes, or even by members of the *petite bourgeoisie*. These were men distinguished from the rest by their intellectual ability, social position or economic security. From their ranks came local preachers and trade union leaders, co-operative pioneers and Chartist agitators, freethinking newsagents and temperance advocates. Such leaders promoted their various agitations for a number of reasons. Some, like the woolcombers of Bradford, felt that their erstwhile secure economic position was being threatened by a new and strange technology, and they rebelled against the whole social system of which it was a part. Others were eager to join chapels and temperance clubs, mechanics' institutes and co-operative stores as a symbol of, and aid to, their advancement

11

in the world. And yet others were frustrated that society did not give them that scope for advancement to which they felt their natural abilities entitled them.

The principal means of communication within the working classes were the newspaper and the public meeting. Both were liable to have legal restrictions imposed on them in times of crisis, the public meeting being especially vulnerable. Communication through the printed word assumed an ability to read, but popular education in the eighteenth century had been largely a matter of rescuing the poor for religion. Sunday schools taught the Bible first and reading only incidentally, although men who could read their Bibles soon learned to read their Thomas Paine pamphlets and their radical newspapers as well. The religious bodies kept a close watch on their schools but they could not control what their pupils read. Even so, most of their scholars could probably not have managed anything which demanded skills beyond the barest literacy. In 1841 33 per cent of the men and 49 per cent of the women married in registry offices could not write their own names (**34, 38**). The national average for 1839–48 was 40 per cent, but with marked regional variations. In general, literacy was highest where the population was most concentrated. *Chambers's Journal* was only being realistic in 1840 when it admitted that it was read by 'the élite of the labouring community; those who think, conduct themselves respectably, and are anxious to improve their circumstances by judicious means. But below this worthy order of men, our work, except in a few particular cases, does not go.'

Working-class leaders and writers on working-class affairs accepted this distinction made between the élite and the residuum of the lower orders. When J. M. Ludlow and Lloyd Jones wrote about the *Progress of the Working Class* (1867), they defined their subject so as to leave out the agricultural workers and the poor. Richard Carlile was quite candid about his policy: 'It is all a mistake about calling in poor men. In appealing to the lowest you do not get them, and by doing so, you shut out the best means of public excitement. . . . The mass of poor men are the sport of every wind, from a tempest to a zephyr' (**2**). One of the earliest atheistical periodicals, the *Investigator* (1843), admitted that it was 'calculated to interest only the intelligent and reasoning portion of the community', and the briefest glance at almost any radical journal would confirm this. 'The masses *cannot* become Secularists until they have opportunities for developing their intellectual and moral faculties' admitted Charles Bradlaugh's *National Reformer* in 1860.

At the same time, literacy and the newspaper-reading habit were spreading in the first half of the nineteenth century (**34**). Men who could not afford a new copy of a paper could buy one secondhand or borrow one, or see one in a public house. Those who could barely read could have others read to them. Men who could do neither could attend public meetings. Those who could not understand abstract ideas could borrow the opinions of their neighbours. This was especially true in the towns of the North: 'The workshop depraves,' wrote Léon Faucher of Manchester in 1844, 'but it throws open to the minds of the operatives a whole world of ideas.' Ludlow and Jones praised the superior intelligence of the workmen of Lancashire and Yorkshire, and Edward Baines made the same point in a speech in 1861. They were thinking not only of the traditional leaders of popular radicalism—the craft workers, artisans, innkeepers and petty shopkeepers—but also of some factory workers, the products of the new industrial system. Channels of communication were wide open between the various ranks of the working class, despite their often different outlooks. One of the most important developments of the century was the political education of all but the lowest in society. Nevertheless, as the Manchester domestic missionary cautioned in 1849, friends of the working class were apt to exaggerate the great intelligence of the working men. The outstanding men were only a tiny minority.

This minority was largely self-educated, and the workman who had educated himself was likely to be highly critical of his former accepted opinions and highly uncritical of his new, self-acquired principles. The radical literature seemed to remove the scales from his eyes, revealing to him the true nature of religion and society. This might inspire him to become a local preacher or a temperance advocate. It inspired others to reject Christianity, and there were strong influences in this latter direction. Anticlericalism and all the other forces of popular protest directed the religious fervour of some working-class leaders into organisations opposed to the churches. 'The devil has got the best long ago,' wrote Charles Kingsley with some exaggeration, 'the cream and the pith of working intellect is almost exclusively self-educated, and therefore, also infidel!' (quoted in **47**). As the nineteenth century progressed, the better-off members of the working class began to discover a new class-consciousness, and to question the social, political and religious world in which they found themselves. Filled with the ideas popularised by Thomas Paine, and led by the publishers of the blasphemous and seditious press, the infidel radicals made a small but influential contribution to most working-class movements of the nineteenth century.

Part Two

DEVELOPMENT

2 The Age of Revolution

THE ORIGINS OF A TRADITION

When Thomas Cooper, the Chartist, lectured on 'The Early English Freethinkers' in 1848, he named among others Lord Herbert of Cherbury, Thomas Hobbes, Charles Blount, John Toland, Lord Shaftesbury, Anthony Collins, Thomas Woolston, Matthew Tindal, Thomas Morgan, Thomas Chubb, Viscount Bolingbroke, Edward Gibbon and David Hume (**9, 27**). These are some of the men who constituted the intellectual ancestry of the nineteenth-century freethinking radicals—men who had little in common with each other except their condemnations of contemporary Christianity on the one hand and their opposition to outright atheism on the other. Some of them were prosecuted for their views, some of them were protected by their social status. In general their influence in Britain was small and their works were not widely read. The English Church was sufficiently flexible to absorb many of the ideas of these deists and was not unduly disturbed by their arguments. No great school of freethinking opinion developed outside the Christian Church.

This was not true of France, where the absolutism of the King in politics and of the Church in matters of religion had promoted a vigorous group of freethinkers. The great names associated with this 'French Philosophy' were, according to a pamphlet of that name published in 1798, those of Voltaire, d'Alembert, Diderot, Turgot, d'Holbach and Rousseau, and to this list should be added the name of Volney, perhaps the most influential of them all. These men, the philosophers of the Enlightenment, had originally taken many of their ideas from England: Voltaire learned his deism from Newton; d'Holbach translated John Toland's *Letters to Serena* (1704) and published them in 1768 as *Lettres Philosophiques*. These French writers developed the philosophy of reason and repaid their debt to England towards the end of the eighteenth century when English translations of their works began to appear. Republicans in France, England and America were then able to draw on a common fund of freethinking literature.

17

In England an 'infidel' or an 'atheist', in the language of the eighteenth and nineteenth centuries, was not necessarily a man who denied the existence of God, but one who had the temerity to convey to the lower orders the heresies of the respectable. The principle by which the authorities acted was that stated by Chief Justice Raymond at the trial of Thomas Woolston (1669–1733) for publishing *Six Discourses on the Miracles of our Saviour* (1727–29): 'Whatever strikes at the very root of Christianity tends manifestly to a dissolution of the Civil Government' (**68**). This statement was generally true, for republicanism and infidelity were often two sides of the same coin. English freethought was born among the sects of the Civil War. John Toland was not only an influential writer against orthodox Christianity, he was also a great republican and Commonwealth's man who published lives of Harrington and Milton. The names associated with the earliest freethought organisations are not those of the great freethinking aristocrats like Shaftesbury, Bolingbroke, Herbert of Cherbury and Molesworth, but of men from the lower orders, like Chubb and Annet. Thomas Chubb (1679–1747), whom Cooper in the lecture cited above described as '*our first working-man freethinker*', was a glover and chandler who belonged to a little debating society in Salisbury, and Peter Annet (1693–1769) was a school teacher who also lectured in the London halls. In 1761 he brought out the *Free Inquirer*, the first freethought journal, in which he was said to have ridiculed the Holy Scriptures and for this he was pilloried, fined, and sentenced to a year's hard labour (**61**).

Annet was a member of the Robin Hood Society—so called because it met at the Robin Hood and Little John inn off the Strand. This society, like the one to which Chubb had belonged, encouraged the discussion of all topics including politics and religion, and it had several imitators in other parts of London (**57**), but these societies were relatively obscure and gained notoriety only in retrospect. It was the French Revolution which set English freethought alight, and what the judges had feared for a hundred years was then proved to be true. The news from France produced a polarisation of attitudes and divided the hitherto moderate reform movement in England. Those who had something to lose rallied to Church and King. Radicalism in religion and politics was forged into a single infidel tradition, and the apostle of this tradition in England, France and America was Thomas Paine.

THOMAS PAINE

Paine (1737–1809) was born in Thetford, Norfolk, the son of a Quaker staymaker (**62, 63**). He was confirmed a member of the Church of England, and even once considered entering that Church's ministry, but his political and religious outlook was long tempered by the attitudes of the Society of Friends. In 1759 he set himself up in Sandwich as a master staymaker, and five years later entered the Excise Service. He was dismissed in 1765 for neglecting his duties, restored to an appointment in Lewes in 1768, and again dismissed for neglect of duty in 1774, though the real reason this time was probably his championing of the Excise officers' demands for more pay. Paine then emigrated to America with letters of introduction from Benjamin Franklin. He soon became involved in the struggles of the American colonies against the government of George III. In his pamphlet, *Common Sense* (1776), he was one of the first to put forward the idea of an independent America, and with his *Crisis* papers (1776–83) he did much to keep up American morale during the war. In 1787 he returned to Europe in an attempt to interest the Parisian Academy of Science in the model of an iron bridge which he had designed. In Paris he met some of the leaders of the Enlightenment and became close friends with Condorcet. Then he returned to England where the outbreak of revolution caught up with him.

Political opposition to the British government in the years before the French Revolution was not confined to the extreme radicals. The Shelburne Whigs, the followers of Wilkes, and many members of the provincial literary and philosophical societies were sympathetic to the cause of reform. The Dissenters, and particularly the Unitarians, were notably outspoken. A sermon by one of the latter, Richard Price (1723–91), to the 'Revolution Society' was the occasion of Edmund Burke's *Reflections on the Revolution in France* (1790) in which Burke seemed to go back on the liberalism with which he had supported the revolution in America and which marked him out as the spokesman for the reaction in England. In reply to Burke, Paine wrote his famous *Rights of Man*. Part 1 of this work, published in 1791, was concerned mainly with France and its constitution. Part 2, written in 1791 and published the following year, concentrated on the follies of the so-called British constitution (**58**). Before the spring was out, an action had been brought against the publisher, and in June Paine himself appeared before the King's Bench, but his trial for sedition was put off until the end of the year. The *Rights of Man* enhanced Paine's republican reputation in France and America, but it made England a dangerous place for him. With Priestley, who had been driven to America by the 'Church and King' mob, and twenty-five others, Paine had been made an honorary French citizen by the Convention, of which he had been elected a member by the Pas de Calais. On the advice of William Blake he therefore left England to take up his seat in September 1792, and in so doing he escaped arrest at Dover by a mere twenty minutes.

In France Paine took part in his second revolution. He was a moderate but was unable to stem the tide. Although a republican he fought for the lives of the King and Queen as private citizens, and although an opponent of the Christian Churches, he was a profoundly religious man. It was against the background of the Terror that Paine wrote his next work, the *Age of Reason*. The manuscript of Part 1 (published 1794), written to prevent the French people from rushing headlong into atheism, was handed to Joel Barlow, the American deist, as Paine was being arrested as an enemy alien. In the Luxembourg prison, awaiting the guillotine, he wrote Part 2 (published 1796) which took the form of a savage attack on the follies and errors of the Bible and of Christianity [**doc. 6**]. This work destroyed Paine's reputation in America, as his *Rights of Man* had previously done in England. He survived the Terror, but when he returned to America in 1802 he found his circle of friends had shrunk to a few extreme Republicans and a handful of American deists. He died amid lies and scandals, in poverty and obscurity, in 1809.

Paine's reputation has always been more extreme than his actual views. In politics he was radical, but not more so than Jefferson or Priestley. In theology he was neither extreme nor original. In fact he was a typical product of the age of reason, a profoundly religious humanistic deist. In Paris he had founded a society of Theophilanthropists—lovers of God and Man—and he described himself as 'a man who considers the world as his home, and the good of it in all places as his object'. His theological opinions were conservative in everything except his rejection of the Christian revelation. He was not a materialist. His arguments were not new. The real roots of his infidelity lie not in his philosophy but in his attacks on the Bible, and in Part 2 of the *Age of Reason* the standard arguments of two generations and more of freethinkers are to be found.

Christian doctrine provided the starting-point. Paine had begun his spiritual pilgrimage with the Atonement, revolting at a doctrine which made 'God Almighty act like a passionate man who killed his son when he could not revenge himself in any other way' (*Age of Reason*, Part 1). This moral revolt led on to the attempt 'to show that the Bible is spurious, and thus, by taking away the foundation, to overthrow at once the whole structure of superstition raised thereon' (*ibid.*, Part 2). The Bible, according to Paine, was incompatible with religion and with nature. It was both muddled and immoral. Incredible legends, such as that describing the fall of Adam, were taken by St Paul as the basis for his theory of the Atonement. The various books of the Bible were written neither at the times supposed nor by the people to whom they were attributed. The good points of its teaching were not new and could be found in the religions of the East.

Here Paine was saying little that Toland, Collins, or Annet had not already said. His significance is that in plain terms he spoke out beyond the literate few and the tiny circle whom the early freethinkers might have reached, to the semiliterate and illiterate many, and he spoke with the twin tongues of infidelity and republicanism at a time of political and social upheaval. Part 1 of the *Rights of Man* went unpunished at the very first because it was initially published at three shillings as a companion volume to Burke's *Reflections*. Part 2 was issued for popular consumption and a case was rapidly brought against its publisher and author. Although Paine managed to escape to France, many publishers of his works were fined and imprisoned and Paine himself was burned in effigy along with copies of his books. The *Rights of Man* was widely sold and read. At the trial of Thomas Walker in 1794, for publishing the *Rights of Man*, evidence was given of the Sheffield Constitutional Society which had republished the offending work at sixpence, and had held public readings of it. The Society for Constitutional Information, to which Paine gave his royalties, had distributed 50,000 copies of Part 1 before the end of 1791, and with the freedom of distribution which Paine gave to all publishers in 1792, four times that number were probably sold in the next two years.

Just as the *Rights of Man* was spread by and inspired a rapid growth in the number of extreme radical organisations, so the *Age of*

Reason encouraged the spread of infidelity by the same channels. W. H. Reid gave his opinion that 'till the *Age of Reason* was adopted by the political societies in this metropolis [London], Deism, to say nothing of Atheism, was rather the affair of a few isolated individuals, than, as it has been since that period, the concern of a considerable part of the community'. Reid was referring in particular to the activities of the London Corresponding Society, 'the sole medium which, for the first time, made infidelity as familiar as possible with the lower orders' (**57, 65**). The society persuaded Thomas Williams to bring out a cheap edition of the work which it distributed to kindred organisations throughout the country. The Bishop of London complained that the *Age of Reason* was being circulated even amongst the miners of Cornwall.

THE REVOLUTIONARY DECADE

The revolution had come to America and France, and was eagerly looked for by the radicals in England, Scotland and Ireland. Political societies were formed to lead the agitation, the most active being the society of United Irishmen, founded in Dublin in 1791, and the London Corresponding Society, founded early the following year. Both spread their organisations to the major centres of population. Sheffield, Manchester and Norwich were among the towns with corresponding societies, and the United Irishmen were influential in Lancashire and Scotland. A 'General Convention of Delegates from Societies of the Friends of the People throughout Scotland' met in Edinburgh in December 1792 and again in April and October 1793. Delegates were received also from London and Ireland, universal suffrage was demanded, and the influence of the French Convention was evident in the proceedings. Revolutionary organisations began to flourish in many towns, and especially among the artisans of London (**12, 64**).

The government was naturally alarmed at this. Two of the Scottish leaders, Thomas Muir and the Reverend T. F. Palmer, were transported in 1793, and following a general meeting called by the London Corresponding Society in April 1794, twelve members of the society were accused of high treason. Three, including Thomas Hardy, the secretary, were tried but all were acquitted. The government then took repressive measures. *Habeas corpus* was suspended, enabling the authorities to detain troublesome people without trial, and, following an attack on the King's coach at the opening of Parliament in 1795, two Bills were introduced. One was to safeguard the King's person and the other placed severe restrictions on the right to hold public meetings. The motive behind these repressive measures was genuine fear. Ireland was seething on the edge of revolt, the navy was mutinous, and the political societies appeared to be in league with the French. Moreover, the extremist society of United Irishmen was beginning to extend its influence in England. Manchester was the centre of activity, but delegates were also sent to London to work through the Corresponding Society. Scotland had its own United Scotsmen. The Irish rebellion of 1798 seemed but the beginning of a genuinely revolutionary move to overthrow the government.

In this world of clubs and corresponding societies, the radical literature was avidly read [**doc. 7**]. Its authorship and attitudes were international. Paine's *Rights of Man* was dedicated to President Washington and to Lafayette. The *Age of Reason* was first published in Paris in both French and English. The most popular works included not only those of Paine but also Godwin's *Political Justice*, Northcote's *Life of David*, and cheap translations of Mirabaud's (*sic*, actually d'Holbach's) *System of Nature*, Volney's *Law of Nature* and *Ruins of Empires*, Voltaire's *Philosophical Dictionary* and Diderot's *Thoughts on Religion*. Discussion groups were formed to consider the ideas put forward by these works. The London Corresponding Society expanded rapidly following the publication of the *Age of Reason* in 1794, and at least one contemporary saw some connection between the two events. Paine was described as 'a man whose writings have made as much noise and produced more conspicuous effects than those of any writer on similar subjects' (**57**). It would be a mistake to give Paine all the credit for the spread of revolutionary activity, but he was its most active and widely read propagandist.

There were parallel developments in France and America. One of the lesser-known clubs in Paris during the revolution was Paine's Republican Society which was responsible for the first open demands for the abolition of the monarchy (1792). The following year, Paine gathered round him in the garden of his house in the Faubourg St Denis a group of like-minded men and women from England and America as well as France. These included Mary Wollstonecraft (wife of William Godwin); Thomas Rickman, the London radical bookseller; Joel Barlow, the American diplomat and translator of Volney's *Les Ruines ou méditation sur les révolutions des empires* (1791); and Nicolas de Bonneville, radical editor and journalist. In 1796 Paine opened a Temple of Reason in Paris as a home for his new religion of Theophilanthropy. Services were held at which humanitarian hymns were sung and ethical readings given from the sacred writings of the Christian, Chinese and Hindu religions (**62**). A similar temple was opened in London in the same year (**57**).

The United States also had its new religion. American deism was the product of a reaction against the strict Puritanism of New England. Its intellectual origins were European, and Elihu Palmer (1764–1806), the most important leader, looked to Locke, Mirabaud, Rousseau, Voltaire, Hume and Bolingbroke. One of the American freethought groups, the 'Newburgh Druids', issued reprints not only of recent works like the *Age of Reason*, but also of one of the pioneering works of English eighteenth-century freethought, Matthew Tindal's *Christianity as Old as Creation* (1730). Palmer himself wrote a *Principles of Nature* which became one of the most popular freethought works of the nineteenth century. In New York a deistical society, later known as the 'Columbian Illuminati', developed out of the local democratic society under Palmer's influence, and a periodical, the *Temple of Reason*, edited by Denis Driscol, was begun in 1800. Palmer divided his time between New York and Philadelphia, where a society of Theophilanthropists had been founded in the same year. When the *Temple of Reason* failed in 1802, Palmer returned to New York intending to build a 'Temple of Nature'. He also started a new periodical, the *Prospect, or View of the Moral World* (1802–05) in which many of Paine's later works were printed (**66**).

All this activity in three countries promised much but achieved little. Theophilanthropy did not catch on. At first, hopes for revolution had been high: the political clubs became more extreme as their membership broadened; England seemed ripe for revolution; Paine urged Napoleon to invade and some radicals began learning French in readiness for the event. But by the end of the century all these hopes were on the wane. The government took stern measures. Paine's first publisher of the *Age of Reason*, Daniel Isaac Eaton, who had already been tried in 1793 for publishing Part 2 of the *Rights of Man*, was tried twice in 1796. He fled to America, his property was confiscated and he was outlawed. When he returned nearly four years later, he was imprisoned for fifteen months. Another publisher,

Thomas Williams, who acted for the London Corresponding Society, was prosecuted in 1797. The case against him was put by Thomas Erskine who had defended the *Rights of Man* in 1792. It was made increasingly more difficult for the radicals to conduct their agitation. The suspension of *Habeas corpus* was annually renewed, seditious meetings had been banned since 1794, the press laws were strengthened against the radical press in 1798 and 1799, corresponding societies were made illegal in 1799, and combinations of workmen were banned by Acts of 1799 and 1800. The London Corresponding Society had already been weakened by internal divisions. Some members had left after the decision to publish the *Age of Reason*, and there was later widespread opposition to the association of the society with the extremist United Irishmen. In 1798 the Irish rebellion was put down. The revolution in France and the United States yielded to conservative forces. Napoleon rose to power in France and brought the republic to an end. He invaded Egypt not England, and by the 1802 Concordat restored the Catholic religion in France. In the United States, the Republican Jefferson was president but the Federalists were using Paine's *Age of Reason* to discredit the left wing of his support. Even Republicans began to avoid Paine's company. The *Prospect* closed in 1805, Palmer died suddenly shortly afterwards, and Paine went to his grave in 1809 (**66**).

Yet the tradition did not die with him, and the work which had been done was not forgotten. The followers of Thomas Spence, to become notorious after the war, were already beginning to organise themselves. The ideas which had been released in the clubs could not be recaptured. W. H. Reid viewed with relief the collapse of political radicalism in 1800, but he concluded his account of the infidel societies with a note of caution: 'Though their meetings are no longer holden,' he warned, 'still, as scattered individuals, they are sufficiently numerous to do considerable mischief; the Atheistical class in particular seem most incorrigible' (**57**).

3 The Blasphemous and Seditious Press

POLITICAL DEVELOPMENTS, 1800–32

Political activity in the first decade of the nineteenth century was subdued but not entirely absent. The Combination Acts of 1799 and 1800, which were designed to prevent trade union activity, were not completely successful. Some workers, especially the skilled artisans, were able to exploit rising prices and war demand to obtain higher wages. Others, such as the stocking weavers of Nottingham and the croppers of the West Riding, found their economic position threatened by new machinery and joined the Luddite movement (**21, 60**).

The end of the war, and the economic depression which accompanied it, produced a revival of political activity equal in intensity to that of the 1790s. The reformers seemed to pick up the threads where they had left off. Major John Cartwright, the veteran reformer of the 1780s, was again active. Hampden clubs and societies for political reform were founded by him as he toured the country (**44a, 59**) Unrest was manifest. In December 1816 the Spenceans (named after Thomas Spence, a poor Newcastle schoolmaster and social reformer) called a meeting at Spa Fields, London, which ended in a riot. As the depression deepened in 1817, the situation became more critical. The government took strong measures and the powers of local magistrates were increased. *Habeas corpus* was again suspended; public meetings were again forbidden. Nevertheless the agitation continued. Starving Manchester handloom weavers and spinners began a march on London, Jeremiah Brandreth led an abortive rising in Derbyshire, and someone threw a stone at the Prince Regent as he drove to open Parliament. The Home Secretary, Lord Sidmouth, was alarmed, though in retrospect he appears to have been the victim of his own imagination which was fed by the exaggerated reports of spies and *agents provocateurs* (**60, 67**).

The economic situation improved in 1818, violence decreased, but radical activity continued. Political Unions were formed during the general election of 1818, and when Burdett's motion for parliamentary reform was defeated by the new Parliament the following year the lull in the agitation came to an end. The situation was made worse by a further onset of the depression in trade. At a massive open-air meeting called by the radical orator, Henry Hunt, in St Peter's Fields, Mnachester, on 16 August 1819, the yeomanry panicked and charged the unarmed crowd. This was the notorious 'Peterloo Massacre' which, more than any other event of the period, stamped the radical movement with bitterness and renewed resolve. The government took even more repressive measures. The Six Acts were passed, three of which arose out of the Peterloo meeting and three of which were concerned with the blasphemous and seditious press [**doc. 9**].

In 1820 the course of reform ran more easily. The alliance of Whig and radical which had been broken since the war, was reformed as both parties used the cause of Queen Caroline as a stick with which to beat both the Tory government and the new king, George IV. The Spenceans plotted in Cato Street to blow up the whole Cabinet, and the Scottish miners and weavers of Bonnymuir attempted a rising, but these were the last two serious occurrences of the type which had characterised the reform movement since the war. Both were inspired by government spies and both were disasters. Thereafter, the most effective way forward lay with the growing co-operative and trade union movements. The Combination Acts were repealed in 1824 and in the next few years the great unions of mid-Victorian England were founded—the North East Miners (1825), the Journeymen Steam Engine Makers (1826), the Carpenters and Joiners (1827) (**24**). John Doherty began to organise his great Spinners Union upon which Robert Owen's schemes were to rest. There was even progress in Parliament. The Duke of Wellington's ultra-Tory government recognised the citizenship of Dissenters (1828) and of Catholics (1829). In 1830 the Tory monopoly of government was finally broken with the formation of a Whig ministry.

The radicals now expected the parliamentary reform for which they had been agitating since the days of John Wilkes. Political Unions were revived, mass meetings were again held, and, in alliance with the middle classes, the working-class leaders scented victory. The Reform Act of 1832 proved a delusion. The true nature of Whig reform had been hinted at in 1830 when the new government had ruthlessly repressed the agricultural labourers. The radical mentality of the 1830s and 1840s cannot be understood unless the shock which the betrayal of 1832 produced is taken into account.

Like Peterloo, it was stored in the memories of the radical working-class leaders as they developed what can be called the beginnings of a class-consciousness (**36, 60**).

THE STRUGGLE, 1816–26

The years immediately after the Napoleonic wars saw the birth of the British radical press. Its pioneer was William Cobbett whose *Weekly Political Register* had been published at 1s 0½d since 1802. In 1816 he decided to issue the leading articles at 2d, and forty thousand copies of the first issue were sold within a month. Henceforward the radical press aimed at a mass readership among the working classes.

The law of the land restricted the press in two ways—legal and financial. The financial regulations went back to the Stamp Act of 1712 which had imposed duties on newspapers, paper, pamphlets and advertisements. By 1815 these 'taxes on knowledge' stood at 4d gross stamp duty on every newspaper, 1s 3d on every almanac, 3s 6d on every advertisement and 3s on each edition of a pamphlet. The Acts of 1798 and 1799 had, in addition, made the registration of printers, publishers, proprietors and presses compulsory. By restricting newspapers to comment only, the radical publishers were able to issue their works as pamphlets, thus paying only the lightest duty, but, in fact, many of the papers strayed over the dividing line between news and comment. The legal restrictions on the press were the laws of libel: defamatory libel against individuals, seditious libel against the political institutions of the country, and blasphemous libel against the institutions of religion (**69, 113**).

Cobbett fled to the United States in 1817 when *Habeas corpus* was suspended, but a new and more extreme generation of radical publishers took his place. William Hone, an antiquarian London bookseller, published a *Reformist's Register* (1817); Jonathan Wooler brought out the *Black Dwarf* (1817–24) and they were followed by many others, starting in London but rapidly spreading through the provinces. To the writers of such papers, nothing was sacred. In defiance of the law and the threats of the government, they freely criticised Church and State. Champion among them in his fearless extremism was Richard Carlile (1790–1843) (**72, 73, 74**).

Carlile was born in Ashburton, Devon, but moved to London in

1813. He did not become involved in radical politics until after the war, when he began to hawk Wooler's *Black Dwarf*, and was soon invited by another London bookseller, W. T. Sherwin, to take over his newspaper and shop in Fleet Street. This he did, and soon ran into trouble. William Hone had been arrested for publishing some political *Parodies* on the Liturgy, Catechism and Prayer Book. Carlile sold these works, was also arrested, and kept in gaol for eighteen weeks until Hone's acquittal released him. While in prison Carlile became more extreme in his views. He read Paine's *Age of Reason* for the first time, and in 1818 demonstrated his new loyalty to Paine by reprinting *Common Sense*, the *Rights of Man* and the *Age of Reason* as well as sixpenny extracts from the writings of other free-thought authors. The *Age of Reason* did not at first sell well, but early in 1819 the Society for the Suppression of Vice began a prosecution which ensured its success. This society had been formed in 1802 and had later merged with the Proclamation Society which had been created in 1787 for a similar purpose and which had been responsible for the original prosecution of the *Age of Reason* in 1797. It was popularly known as the Vice Society and was associated with such leading Evangelical statesmen as William Wilberforce.

By the summer of 1819, Carlile had nine cases pending against him. Then came Peterloo. Carlile was present and wrote a devasta-ting account of it. He was charged with seditious libel, but tried in October for blasphemy. The first three days of the trial were taken up with the *Age of Reason* case. Carlile insisted on reading out in court the whole of the offending book, to ensure that it would have an increased and legal circulation in the *verbatim* report of the trial. He was, as expected, found guilty and sentenced to a £1,000 fine and two years in prison for selling the *Age of Reason* and a £500 fine and a year in prison for selling Palmer's *Principles of Nature*. In addition, he had to provide securities for his own good behaviour for life. He was unable to provide any of the money and so was sent to Dorchester gaol for an indefinite stay.

Carlile's aim had been publicity, and he got it. The weekly circulation of the *Republican*, as Carlile had renamed Sherwin's paper in August 1819, rose to fifteen thousand during the trial. Two thousand copies of the *Age of Reason* were sold in six months and the *First Day's Proceedings of the Mock Trial of Richard Carlile* sold ten thousand twopenny numbers.

The Six Acts, which were passed towards the end of 1819, added to the government's powers to deal with the situation. Magistrates were given greater powers to enforce the law against blasphemous and seditious publications, and the financial restrictions on the press were increased. Henceforward, small cheap papers issued more frequently than once a month were brought within the terms of the Stamp Acts [**doc. 9**]. The cheap press could no longer claim exemption by cutting out all the news and so it was killed. The *Black Dwarf* went up to sixpence; Carlile's *Republican* was doubled in size and also went up to sixpence.

After Peterloo a new wave of prosecutions began, chiefly aimed at Carlile's work. The government's policy was to suppress the men who sold the blasphemous and seditious papers. Twenty-five informations were laid against ten London booksellers in 1819, and many leading provincial radicals were broken for selling the *Black Dwarf*, the *Republican*, Hone's *Parodies* and other extreme publications. But the government was fighting a losing battle. Hone followed up his *Parodies* with *The Political House that Jack Built*, which ran to fifty editions by the end of 1820, selling a hundred thousand copies, and in 1820 he parodied the speech from the throne in *The Man in the Moon*. The law could not touch works like this. As Hone's acquittal in 1817 had shown, to prosecute wit merely brought the government into even greater ridicule.

Carlile was in Dorchester prison from November 1819 to November 1825, but this did not stop his work. First his wife, then his sister, kept the shop open, selling the *Republican* and works by and about Paine, but by the end of 1821 all three members of the Carlile family were in Dorchester gaol. The *Republican* closed, but not for long. A relay of shopmen from all over the country kept Carlile's business open and active [**doc. 10**].

The Society for the Suppression of Vice was joined in 1820 by a secular counterpart, the Constitutional Association (usually known to radicals as the Bridge Street Gang). This Association commenced a number of prosecutions against London and provincial radicals, especially those who worked for Carlile. Their method was to threaten the booksellers with the heavy costs of a trial and to disrupt their businesses by having the accused imprisoned while awaiting trial. In this way the Association could achieve its ends even if it could not always obtain convictions or sentences—and in the first two years of its existence the Association won only four convictions, only one case actually being carried through to sentence.

In 1822 the Bridge Street Gang was more successful. Carlile's *Republican* was restarted and well supplied with contributions from gaol. The Association proceeded against the men in the shop and brought about its closure in February. New premises were soon found and business was recommenced after only six weeks [**doc. 10**]. *The Report of the First Day's Proceedings* was completed and sold; a 1s 6d edition of the *Age of Reason* was published; the Koran was issued in threepenny numbers. As the prosecutions continued more volunteers came from the provinces to fill the gaps. One such man was James Watson (1799–1874), who was to become the leading radical publisher of the next generation (**80**). Watson was a Yorkshireman, who had first become involved in radical politics when he went to the radical reformers' room in Briggate, Leeds, in 1818. There he had seen copies of Wooler's *Black Dwarf* and Cobbett's *Register*, and had met several of the men who, like himself, were to go to London to help Carlile. He arrived in 1823 and helped Mrs Carlile on her release to open a new shop in the Strand, but shortly afterwards he was himself imprisoned for a year for selling Palmer's *Principles of Nature*. The business was then moved back to Fleet Street and the next eight months were relatively quiet, for the Constitutional Association had been discredited, and both it and the Vice Society were short of funds. The Home Secretary, Robert Peel, had been obliged to take matters into his own hands, and Watson was prosecuted directly by the government.

In May 1824 the Home Office made its last assault. Within three weeks eleven arrests were made. Fleet Street was emptied and Newgate filled. Three of the shopmen—William Campion, Richard Hassall and Thomas Riley Perry—issued their own *Newgate Monthly Magazine or calendar of men, things, and opinions*. The government realised that such men were irrepressible, so Peel began to modify his policy. Carlile was unconditionally released in November 1825, and by the end of 1826 only three men were left in prison. The *Republican* was then brought to an end, and one stage in Carlile's life was over.

What had been achieved? Little of positive value can be pointed to. No English laws were changed, but the system of fines and sureties was amended so that, in practice, they became commutative. This meant that a man was no longer liable to indefinite imprisonment if he could not pay his fines or would not give sureties for good behaviour. Carlile's victory was that he successfully claimed the right of the press to criticise freely the institutions of Church and State. Many more battles were to be fought before this right was finally won, but in these years the government was shown that ruthless repression was self-defeating (**68**).

CARLILE AND TAYLOR

Carlile had started out as a political reformer but he became increasingly involved in religious questions. He rejected the deism he had learned from Paine while he was in Dorchester gaol, and his *Address to Men of Science* (May 1821) clearly sets out his changed opinions [**doc. 11**]. The new approach was reflected in the *Republican* when it reappeared in 1822. 'There is no such a God in existence as any man has preached; nor any kind of God', he wrote. While in gaol he had come to put less and less faith in purely political reform, but instead looked to education and the power of the press. After 1826 he changed his position again. His materialism began to give way to mysticism. Carlile the radical political reformer became Carlile the radical moral reformer. His partner in this new crusade was one of the strangest characters in the whole freethought movement, the Reverend Robert Taylor (1784–1844) (**78, 79**).

Taylor had trained as a surgeon and as a clergyman in the Church of England, but he had become a deist after reading Paine and Gibbon. After several attempts to re-enter the Church in the Isle of Man and in Ireland, he returned to London and in November 1824 began a long series of public meetings in which he reviewed the standard 'Christian evidences' put forward by men like William Paley. Then, in 1827, he delivered thirty-eight ethical treatises followed by discussions in the Areopagus coffee house, in which he sought to demolish the foundations of the Scriptures. The City authorities decided to put a stop to this open infidelity and Taylor was charged with blasphemy, committed, and sentenced to a year in Oakham gaol.

The prosecution of Taylor was a cause close to Carlile's heart. In January 1828 he had started a new periodical, the *Lion*, in which he printed the texts of Taylor's lectures. Taylor contributed a weekly prison letter, and while at Oakham also wrote two major books. One of them, the *Syntagma*, was a reply to a fundamentalist Christian critic, the Reverend John Pye Smith. The other, the *Diegesis*, was a long and learned work in which Taylor drew on the whole breadth and depth of his knowledge to disprove the claims of Christianity. The principal thesis of the book was that Christianity had its roots not in historical fact but in the same mythologies which had given birth to the other religions of the East. The work became a free-thought classic. On his release from Oakham in 1829, Taylor went to live with Carlile, and in May the two men commenced an infidel mission to the provinces.

Ever since the *Republican* had been restarted in 1822, Carlile had been building round its sale and distribution little groups of followers throughout the country. These Zetetic societies, as they were called, often provided the local leadership for radical movements in general and for the free press struggles in particular. Carlile and Taylor began their mission to such societies by fastening a thesis on the door of the University Library, Cambridge. They then progressed through Wisbech, Stamford, Nottingham, Leeds, Bradford, Manchester, Ashton, Bolton, Stockport, Liverpool, Wigan, Blackburn, Bury, Hyde and Huddersfield, before returning to London for the winter. They met with some opposition, particularly in the hiring of halls; their lectures were not always well received, but in Liverpool and Huddersfield they reported great success. A similar mission was proposed for the following year, but Carlile developed other plans.

In May 1830 he acquired the use of a lecture hall near Blackfriars Bridge, which was known as the Rotunda. In this place, Taylor gave a series of lectures on the Bible, which were later published in a periodical entitled the *Devil's Pulpit*. Carlile also started a new journal, the *Prompter*, in which he defended the agricultural labourers' revolt of 1830. For this he was indicted on a charge of seditious libel, found guilty, and in January 1831 sentenced to two years in prison and a fine of £200. He did not pay the fine, and was imprisoned for a further eight months. In July 1831 Taylor also was tried, on account of two blasphemous lectures he had delivered the previous Easter [**doc. 12**]. He was imprisoned for two years and fined £100. Although both men were now in prison, the Rotunda was not closed. On Paine's birthday, 29 January 1832, 'A Lady from the Country' began to lecture there, or rather she read lectures written for her by either Carlile or Taylor. This woman was Eliza Sharples (usually known as Isis). She had heard Carlile when he had visited the North on the 1829 mission, had been converted by him, and had followed him to London. With the help of Julian Hibbert and John

Gale Jones she kept the Rotunda open until March and then moved to a lecture room attached to Carlile's shop in Bouverie Street.

Imprisonment was really the end of Taylor. The year after his release he married a rich admirer, and retired to Jersey where he died in 1844. Carlile was not silenced, but he was a changed man. Under the influence of Taylor and with the guidance of Eliza Sharples, he completed his conversion to a mystical interpretation of what he now called Christianity. In a new periodical, the *Isis*, he announced in May 1832: 'I declare myself a convert to the truth as it is in the gospel of Jesus Christ', though what he meant by 'truth' was still highly unorthodox. He had by this time been estranged from his wife for some years, and so he took this opportunity to announce a 'spiritual union' between himself and Eliza Sharples. Henceforward they lived as man and wife.

The *Isis* was concluded at the end of 1832, and replaced by the *Gauntlet* in which Carlile attacked the Political Unions, disagreed with the Owenites, sympathised with Ireland, and supported educational reform. In 1834 the *Gauntlet* gave way to the *Scourge*, and Carlile found himself in prison again. This time he had retaliated against the collectors of church rates by erecting the effigies of a bishop and a distraining officer in the window of his Fleet Street shop. He later added a devil arm in arm with the bishop. For causing a public nuisance he was prosecuted and spent the next four months in gaol. Whilst there he wrote an open letter to Sir Robert Peel on *Church Reform*, in which he advocated a regeneration of the Church as a 'School of Moral Sciences', and he spent the rest of his life agitating for this. His attitude is indicated by the titles of his last three periodicals: the *Church, Carlile's Railroad to Heaven* and the *Christian Warrior*. He took out a licence to preach and toured the provinces (**74**). He opened a Hall of Science in Manchester in 1838, and took over the Bristol Hall of Science from the Owenites in 1842, the year before his death. He was active to the end but was out of touch with the radical movement of which he had once been a leader.

THE UNSTAMPED PRESS

Carlile had challenged the legal restrictions on the press. There still remained the financial. The cheap press had been driven out of existence in 1819. In the 1830s it made a comeback, assisted by the middle-class radicals. The political situation called into being a new radical press which chafed under the restrictions of 1819 (**69, 77**). The Society for the Diffusion of Useful Knowledge petitioned Parliament. A 'victim fund' was organised with George Birkbeck (the pioneer of the mechanics' institutions) and Francis Place as treasurers, and William Lovett and James Watson as secretaries. The first victim was William Carpenter, and after his imprisonment Henry Hetherington continued the agitation (**76**).

Hetherington was born in London and trained as a printer. In the 1820s he was a member of the Freethinking Christians sect, but broke with them over their attitude to the Jews. He was also a founder member of the London Mechanics' Institute. On Christmas Day 1830 he issued the first of a series of separate papers, each one headed differently, but each one written by 'the Poor Man's Guardian'. For one of these papers, entitled the *Republican*, he was brought to court. Thereafter he abandoned all pretence and issued an unstamped penny weekly called the *Poor Man's Guardian*, 'to try the power of *Might* against *Right*'. The government used all its powers to suppress the paper but, in the spirit of the Carlile agitation ten years before, Hetherington refused to give way. He was twice imprisoned for six months—on the first occasion he became a deist. His presses were seized; parcels of papers were confiscated; his street-hawkers were punished; but the *Poor Man's Guardian* continued. In 1833 he began a second paper, the *People's Conservative*, which was also brought to the notice of the courts. Hetherington was fined a further £120 in 1834, but Baron Lyndhurst at the Exchequer ruled that the 1819 Act applied only to newspapers which were like the sevenpenny newspapers. The *Conservative* was therefore illegal, but the *Guardian* was not.

The decision was a great step forward, and to some extent restored the situation before 1819, but the notorious Stamp Acts still stood. The radicals pressed hard for repeal. John Arthur Roebuck, M.P. for Bath, began a weekly series of supposedly individual pamphlets, as had Carpenter and Hetherington before him. A vigorous agitation was conducted both inside and outside Parliament. A committee was formed which later became the London Working Men's Association, the forerunner of Chartism. The agitation brought many of the leading Chartists together, including Bronterre O'Brien, G. J. Harney, Hetherington, Watson and Lovett (**97**).

In 1836 the government made a concession. The newspaper stamp was reduced to a penny—low enough to take the sting out of the agitation but high enough to hamper the development of the radical press. The stamp was not made optional for another twenty years, and the last of the restrictions on the press did not go until 1869. The agitation for complete repeal continued to be the special work of the infidel radicals.

THE TRADITION

In these twenty years between the end of the Napoleonic Wars and the reduction of the stamp duty, the writers and publishers of the blasphemous and seditious press had made great progress. They had established the tradition of Thomas Paine. If the decade of the French Revolution can be called the childhood of the British radical movement, then this was the time of its adolescence. The radical publishers handed the philosophy of the Enlightenment down to the nineteenth century. Shortly after Carlile's release from gaol a public dinner was held on Paine's birthday, 29 January 1826, at which toasts were drunk to Paine, Owen, Rousseau, Voltaire, Diderot, d'Holbach, Benjamin Franklin, Elihu Palmer, Tindal, Toland, Annet, Tillotson, Conyers Middleton, Byron, Shelley and 'all Englishmen who have written to the end of human improvement' (**36**). 'The writings of Thomas Paine,' wrote Carlile in 1821, 'alone, form a standard of anything worthy of being called Radical Reform' (**60**). And so it was to be. Carlile had republished Paine, Volney, Palmer, d'Holbach, and Peter Annet's *Free Inquirer* of 1761. Taylor had provided in his *Diegesis* a standard textbook of scholarly arguments against historical Christianity. Carlile's publications were spread far and wide. 'The writings of Carlile and Taylor and other infidels are more read than the Bible or any other book', a Bolton manufacturer told the Select Committee on Hand-loom Weavers' Petitions in 1834 (**60**). A Manchester town missionary in 1840 reported that he had visited one poor man who 'had been drawn into the vortex of infidelity by the vile trash which came from the pen of Carlile'. Fourteen years later another missionary was recommended by one man he visited to read Paine's *Age of Reason* which he had by him in a bookcase. Carlile had in his possession a plaster-cast statue of Paine. This later became the property of James Watson, who in turn offered it to Joseph Cowen (**4**). The continuity is significant.

But Carlile was not typical. His influence at the time was probably less than Cobbett's, whose religious opinions may best be described as middle-of-the-road, commonsense Anglican (**23**). Carlile quarrelled with most of the other radical leaders. He attacked Cobbett, the Political Unions and the Chartists. William Lovett said he supported Carlile, Taylor and Watson not because he agreed with them but because 'they helped to establish the right *of all men* to honestly declare and publish their opinions regarding what they believe to be right and true' (**89**). Cobbett gave a similar reason for supporting Carlile, although he deplored the offensive blasphemy of the *Republican*. Even the other radical booksellers found Carlile difficult to get on with, and Carlile later claimed that in 1827 Hetherington, Cleave and Carpenter had formed an association from which they had publicly and specifically excluded him (**2**). Carlile's influence was strictly limited, as was that of all the infidel radicals. Lord Holland said in the debate on the Libels Bill in 1819 that the religious as well as the infidel press was expanding at this time, and so many Methodist and Evangelical tracts were being circulated 'as to make religious enthusiasm rather than infidelity the national characteristic' (**68**). Carlile's *Prompter* in 1830 sold only a thousand copies, three-quarters of these in London. But by this time his star was on the wane. The infidel leadership was passing to the men whose schemes he criticised but whose Rational Religion was similar to his own. These men were the followers of the social gospel of Robert Owen.

4 The New Moral World

ROBERT OWEN AND OWENISM

Robert Owen was born in Newtown, Montgomery, in 1771, and died in the same place eighty-seven years later, but he did not belong to rural Wales. He made his way through the drapery business from humble shopboy in Stamford to cotton factory master in Manchester, and then went on to become manager and part-owner of the New Lanark mills in Scotland before he was thirty (**93, 94**). Many of the early cotton factories were more than a collection of mills—they had also to include houses for the workers, and institutional dwellings for the pauper children on whose labour the factories so often depended —and New Lanark was no exception. While there, Owen began to work out his ideas about how a community should be built, and he put into practice some of the plans current at the time in books like William Godwin's radical and popular *Political Justice*, which emphasised that environment had an overwhelming influence on the formation of character, and that education in its fullest sense was indispensable to the wellbeing of any community (**36, 97**). So when Owen took on the management of the New Lanark mills in 1800, he also became public health inspector, housing officer and, above all, educator in his little community (**95**).

Owen did not give formal expression to his views until 1813, when he published his first *Essay on the Formation of Character* which announced the essence of all his theories:

> Any general character, from the best to the worst, from the most ignorant to the most enlightened, may be given to any community, even to the world at large, by the application of the proper means; which means are to a great extent at the command and under the control of those who have influence in the affairs of men (**90**).

This was a paternalistic doctrine, and Owen looked to the government to implement his theories, especially with a view to solving the problem of the poor in the postwar depression (1815–20). He proposed communities in which men and women could live and work in idyllic bliss, exchanging their products, not at market price, but at a price related to the quantity of labour expended on each product. His views were sympathetically heard but were ignored in practice by those in authority.

Other men were more favourable. The Laird of Dalzell offered to implement the scheme, and a community was actually begun at Orbiston, near Motherwell. J. S. Vandaleur later handed over his Irish estate at Ralahine to E. T. Craig who managed it for a time on community lines. Some radicals, such as Cobbett, were sceptical, but a group of working men—most of them printers, and including Hetherington—formed a London Co-operative and Economical Society in 1821 to plan a community, and some efforts were made at communal dwelling in Spa Fields (**93, 95, 98**).

Owen knew of these schemes, but did not think highly of them. He regarded them as too modest to be of any real significance, and so emigrated to America in the hope of finding a more favourable environment for his new society. The community he founded at New Harmony, Indiana, broke on the rocks of individualism, however, and in 1829 he returned to England to find that the paternalistic seeds which he had sown were beginning to bear surprisingly demo-cratic fruits. The attempt to form communities had given way to less ambitious schemes centred on trading stores. In 1827 stores had been opened in London and Brighton. The first storekeeper for the London co-operators was James Watson, and he was succeeded in 1829 by William Lovett. The co-operative idea spread and the journal of the Brighton co-operators was widely read, inspiring stores throughout the industrial North. When Watson went to visit his Yorkshire relatives in 1830, he addressed meetings of co-operators in Leeds, Halifax, Dewsbury, Huddersfield and Wakefield. William Pare of Birmingham and Alexander Campbell of Glasgow were similarly occupied in lecturing to the new groups.

The early co-operators were concerned with production as well as consumption, and so, although Owen despised the stores, he took an interest in the new movement as a means of implementing his labour theory of value. Exchange Bazaars had been opened at which goods could be bought and sold for 'labour notes' (i.e. notes valued not in £1 units but in labour hours), and in 1832 Owen opened his own National Equitable Labour Exchange in London. For a time it was successful, but a backlog of less desirable items, coupled with a dispute about the tenancy of the Exchange building, brought the experiment to an end (**93**).

Among the principal supporters of the Exchanges were the trade unions and so Owen turned to these next. John Doherty, who had built up the Cotton Spinners Union in the 1820s, had extended his horizon to include the Staffordshire potters in 1830. Meanwhile the Birmingham builders were organising themselves, and in 1833 formed a Grand National Guild. Owen perceived the vast potential power which the workers had through industrial action, and he rallied the forces of unionism under the banner of the Grand Moral Union of the Productive Classes. Early in 1834 this became the Grand National Consolidated Trades Union (**95**).

This union did not last long. Sectional strikes broke the united front, and the employers enforced a document whereby their men had to renounce the union to secure employment. Like Owen's other plans, the union appeared to have failed, but it left its mark.

Through the stores and the unions of the 1820s and 1830s, Owenism became the ideology of the leaders of the working classes, and it remained such until the end of the nineteenth century. No working-class movement, especially in the industrial North, could escape its influence, and in London the leaders of the radical movements were, in varying degrees, followers of Robert Owen. The London Co-operative Trading Association became, successively, the Society for the Promotion of Co-operative Knowledge (1829), the British Association for the Promotion of Co-operative Knowledge (1830), and the National Union of the Working Classes (1831). Its original members included Watson, Hetherington, Cleave and Lovett, with O'Brien joining shortly afterwards. These men were not only the leaders of the free press struggle, they were also the pioneers of 'knowledge' Chartism (**97**). Owen was not their leader but he was their prophet. He accepted the commonplaces of eighteenth-century rationalist thought and passed them on to the nineteenth-century radical leaders. His influence was so great because, in the words of his own doctrine, they were the product of the same circumstances as he, and so they were predisposed to believe what he told them. Not least was this true of his religious opinions.

RELIGION

Owen was not against religion as such, but his dogmatic way of speaking often gave the contrary impression. His opposition to religion was based on the fact that so often it seemed to produce division among men instead of harmony. He had the rationalist's contempt for sectarianism, and found the orthodox and religious stumbling blocks in the way of progress. This explains the attitude he adopted when he addressed a series of meetings at the London Tavern in 1817. On 21 August he undertook to answer the question 'If the new arrangements proposed really possess all the advantages that have been stated, why have they not been adopted in universal practice, during all the ages which have passed?' His reply was that mankind had been blinded by the errors of religion or, as he later qualified it, superstition (**90**) [**doc. 14**].

Owen subsequently overdramatised the importance of this speech. It is true that he had taken the opportunity to express in the open views he had long been suspected of holding in private, and that his heretical opinions were used to discredit the cause of factory reform which he had championed, but in most other things the old immoral world continued along its usual course. The Duke of Kent put the speech in context as a plea for religious toleration (**99**), and Owenism itself was not instantly regarded as infidelity, except in so far as certain individuals, such as Wilberforce, were predisposed to treat Owen as an infidel (**92**). Complaints about Owen's theological opinions did not become widespread for another ten years. In 1827 the *Co-operative Magazine* deplored his 'religiophobia', and the really significant declaration of Owen's views did not come until 1829 when he held a much publicised debate with the Reverend Alexander Campbell in New Orleans. The first proposition of this debate gives the flavour of the whole: 'That all religions are founded on the ignorance of mankind' (**93**). William Lovett later wrote that 'The question of *religion* was not productive of much dissension until Mr Owen's return from America' (**89**). It was then that Owen began to hold public meetings on Sunday mornings at the London Tavern, at which speakers from the floor included the notorious Robert Taylor. The Owenites used many of the same buildings as the followers of Carlile and Taylor, and shared much of the same membership, so they were often confused in the public mind. It was

at this time, when Owenism became associated with a mass movement among the working classes, that Owen's views were branded as
'infidel'. His infidelity lay not so much in what he said as in the fact
that he shared these views with the radical leaders at a time of
political unrest.

This identification of the co-operative movement with the private
views of the garrulous philanthropist, was annoying to many
co-operators, particularly the patrons who had built up the movement in Owen's absence, and the 1832 Co-operative Congress tried
to dissociate the movement from any particular theological views.
The decision was a dead letter, for many of the rank-and-file
co-operators had been prepared by Paine and Carlile to find in
Owen's views a reflection of their own beliefs.

Two of Owen's doctrines were regarded as being especially
wicked. One, that of moral non-responsibility, followed on from
Owen's emphasis on the importance of circumstances in the formation of character: it led to a denial 'that Man is bad by nature,
and that he can believe or disbelieve, feel or not feel, as he pleases;
that he forms his own character, and that, consequently, he ought
to be rewarded or punished for it, both in this world and the world to
come' (**92**). This denial arose directly out of the eighteenth-century
humanist attitude towards man, and, like the natural-law theories of
the Enlightenment, it ruled out human free will, and contradicted
the teachings of orthodox Christianity, as emphasised by the
Evangelicals, on original sin, redemption and salvation by faith.
The second wicked and immoral doctrine was that concerning
marriage and divorce, and the problem of sexual freedom. The freethinking radicals were involved in the beginnings of the agitation for
birth control by artificial means. Owen was said to have brought
back from Paris a paper on the subject, Carlile had published
contraceptive advice in the *Lion*, and Owen's son, Robert Dale,
had published a pamphlet on birth control entitled *Moral Physiology*
in 1830. Five years later, Owen delivered a series of lectures on
'The Marriages of the Priesthood of the Old Immoral World' in
which he advocated divorce on the grounds that individuals, having
no free will, could not continue loving their partners if circumstances
changed during the course of marriage. The version of the lectures
which the public read was expressed in more extreme terms. Readers
who were confident that Owenism meant immorality were not
surprised that the printed version of the lectures reported Owen as

describing marriage as 'a Satanic device of the Priesthood to place and keep mankind within their slavish superstitions, and to render them subservient to all their purposes' (**93, 99**).

After the collapse of the Grand National Consolidated Union in 1834 Owenism was reduced to its true sectarian proportions. It had always had the characteristics of a religious body. Owen denounced religion with true religious zeal, and his writings provided a new gospel. His communities were similar to, and drew inspiration from, those of religious groups like the Shakers and Rappites. Owen was a prophet and he proclaimed his new moral world with millenarian fervour. After 1834 these sectarian characteristics became even more pronounced. His organisations became religious bodies, and his followers drew in on themselves to preserve their purity from the world. They acquired buildings and their lecturers took out licences to preach. Owenism had influenced and continued to influence working-class thought, but it could no longer command a mass movement. Owen turned his back on the past, and abandoned the petty details of co-operation. Socialism was henceforth to be his mission.

SOCIALISM

Owen left the rapidly declining Grand National Consolidated Trade Union in 1834, and in the autumn of that year started a new body called the British and Foreign Consolidated Association of Industry, Humanity and Knowledge. In 1835 this became the Association of All Classes of All Nations, which was to prepare public opinion for the coming of the 'new moral world'. This phrase was adopted as the title for a new periodical, started in November 1834. The new society made a slow start, especially in London, where the radical leaders were showing more interest in political reform than in the latest schemes of the 'Social Father', as Owen was known, but the embers of enthusiasm for Owen's schemes had never entirely died out in the North, and Owen was able to fan them into flames once more. A Congress was held in Manchester in 1837, at which the affairs of the Association were put on a regular basis. A Central Board was elected to administer the Association, with G. A. Fleming, editor of the *New Moral World*, as general secretary, and a second society was formed, the National Community Friendly Society, to raise funds for a socialist experiment. Also at this Congress, the Owenites officially described themselves as 'Socialists', and appointed two 'social missionaries' to assist Owen to propagate his gospel. In the next twelve months, the number of local branches of the Association increased from three to thirty-two. Congress was again held in Manchester in 1838, when six missionaries were appointed, and by the time of the next Congress (Birmingham, 1839) fifty-nine local branches had been formed. The movement was gaining momentum, so Owen began to make further plans. The Association of All Classes and the Community Society were amalgamated to form the Universal Community Society of Rational Religionists (or Rational Society, for short), and an estate of 530 acres was leased in the parish of East Tytherly, Hampshire. Meanwhile, the local branches were beginning to build 'Social Institutions' or 'Halls of Science' in which to hold their meetings (**6, 95**).

The government did not appear unduly disturbed at this spread of Socialism. The Home Secretary was more worried about Chartist disturbances, and the Prime Minister, Lord Melbourne, had even gone so far as to allow Owen to present a petition in person to the Queen. The religious leaders of the country were not so complaisant. Local clergymen were alarmed at the spread of infidel Socialism, and their fears were voiced in Parliament by Henry Philpotts, the Tory Bishop of Exeter [**doc. 17**]. He bombarded the Lords with the petitions of pious subjects, accused the Socialists of breaking the Seditious Meetings Act of 1817, charged them with wanting to abolish private property, marriage and religion, and denounced the government for neglecting the safety of the country. The Whigs, he declared, had allowed Civil Marriage (1837) and then appointed the Socialist leader, William Pare, as the first civil registrar of Birmingham; they had passed the Municipal Corporations Act (1835) and the mayor of the reformed corporation of Coventry was showing unheard-of favouritism towards the Socialists. Melbourne was unmoved, so the Bishop continued his attack. Finally, the Home Secretary sent a letter to be read at all Quarter Sessions commanding magistrates to search for blasphemous and seditious literature. Hetherington, Cleave, and Heywood of Manchester were accused of selling C. J. Haslam's *Letters to the Clergy of All Denominations* (1840). Hetherington and Watson began countercharges against four respectable London booksellers for selling Shelley's *Queen Mab*, which William Clarke had been prosecuted for publishing in 1821. The case against Heywood was therefore dropped, Cleave's prison sentence was remitted, and no action was taken against Hetherington until Philpotts complained, whereupon Hetherington was given the lightest possible sentence (**76, 80**).

The Socialists thrived on persecution, which was why the government had tried to avoid it. The 1841 Congress was told that, in the previous year, fifty formal discussions had been held with the clergy, nearly 1,500 lectures had been given (over 600 of them on theological and ethical subjects), and 350 towns had been regularly visited by fourteen missionaries and lecturers (**6**). Halls of Science were being built or leased in most large towns, the East Tytherly community (usually known as Queenwood, after the principal farm on the estate) was beginning to take shape, and a group of unofficial Owenites had already started a community at Manea Fen in Cambridgeshire. Whatever the government thought, local clergymen and their supporters could not tolerate such activity. John Brindley, master of the National School at March, near Manea, began a lecture tour against the Socialists. Wherever he went, by exaggerating the immoral tendencies of Socialism, he was able to call up mob violence against the Owenites. In the Potteries, employers dismissed Owenites from their works, and in Bristol, at the opening of the Hall of Science, a riot occurred which wrecked the interior fittings of the newly decorated hall (**92**). Nonconformist ministers painted lurid pictures of what the Socialists were like [**doc. 16**]. The incumbent of St Matthias's Church, Manchester, was appalled to find that he had a new Hall of Science virtually on his doorstep [**doc. 18**]. The hall was opened on 1 June 1840, and within ten days the three door stewards were being charged with taking money in a public hall on a Sunday, contrary to the Treasonable and Seditious Practices Act of 1799. The Socialists defended themselves by pleading, in vain, that their hall was registered as 'intended to be used as a place of religious worship, by an assembly of protestants, called rational religionists'. A further charge was therefore brought, that Owen and two of his lecturers, James Rigby and Robert Buchanan, were not licensed to preach in a place of religious worship. Owen and Rigby lived beyond the jurisdiction of the court, but Buchanan was compelled to take the oath of a dissenting preacher (*N.M.W.* 4, 11 July, 1 August 1840) (**6**).

This action forced the Socialists to decide what their attitude was towards religion. By his actions, Owen had implied that he thought it necessary to attack religion, and in 1837 he had resumed his practice, started in 1829, of debating the merits of the Christian religion in public, but the following year he changed his mind and instructed his missionaries not to involve themselves in theological controversy. Most of the lecturers seem to have ignored him. For example, Henry Jeffery found the branch at Edinburgh 'a hybrid, unitarian kind of concern' which regarded Socialism as being 'genuine, primitive, practical, or some other sort of Christianity', but he soon introduced the 'strong meat' of irreligion and thereby increased the membership of the branch (Jeffery to Holyoake, 7 April 1842) (2). At Queenwood John Finch, the deputy-governor, lectured against Christianity on Sunday afternoons [doc. 17], and in Manchester Robert Cooper critically analysed the Holy Scriptures, but the Central Board supported Owen. Another social missionary, Lloyd Jones, took the oath, and the editor of the *New Moral World* regarded it as a mere formality. The Liverpool social missionary was told that he would be dismissed if he did not stop speaking against Christianity.

The Central Board had good reason for its point of view, but it was a reason which infuriated many Owenites. Robert Owen was not the man to be content with slow progress towards something less than the millennium. His career is marked by sudden enthusiasms followed by equally sudden periods of cooling off. He had supported the labour exchanges until the trade unions had come along. He had devoted all his energies to these, until he glimpsed the wider vision of the new moral world. He had been enthusiastic about the Association of All Classes, but by 1840 his energies were being diverted into the effort to build a working model of the new society at Queenwood. Unlike the earlier community experiments in Britain this one had Owen's full backing, so it had to be on the grandest scale. Nothing was to be spared, for it was to demonstrate once and for all the practicability of Owen's schemes and the truth of his principles.

This needed money. In order to raise funds, Owen founded in 1840 a Home Colonisation Society, with William Galpin, Frederick Bate and Henry Travis as wealthy supporters. The major concern of the Central Board was to placate these influential men. Galpin became secretary of the Central Board, and Owen appeared to have reverted to the 'philanthropy at five per cent' of his early New Lanark days. The local leaders of Socialism, struggling to keep up their mortgage payments on their Halls of Science, did not like it. An appeal was launched in 1842 for a million pounds, and the Congress of 1842 took steps to encourage contributors. The powers of local branch members were severely curtailed, social missionaries were subjected to the control of the Central Board and not to Congress, and the Queenwood Community was taken out of the hands of the ordinary members and put in trust on behalf of the creditors. Despite these measures, the money was not forthcoming. The income of 1842 did not even meet ordinary expenditure, but huge sums were lavished on the community for a dwelling house hopefully named 'Harmony Hall'. The scheme gradually bled the propagandist organisation to death (**6,** 21, 28 May 1842).

In 1844 the ordinary members of the Rational Society rebelled. John Finch of Liverpool was elected Chairman of Congress instead of Owen, who consequently resigned as president of the Society. John Buxton of Manchester was elected in his place, and also as governor of Harmony Hall. This revolution provoked a further crisis in confidence and accelerated the collapse of the Society's shaky affairs. The next Congress assigned the property to Buxton, Bate and George Bracher, to dispose of as they saw fit. The trustees, led by John Finch, claimed that they alone could dispose of the property. Finch ejected Buxton from the Hall, and in 1846 a Congress was held by his tent at the roadside (**93**). The grand schemes had collapsed amid confusion, mistrust and bitterness. A remnant gathered at the London headquarters of Socialism, the John Street Institution, but could muster only 187 members. The quarrel between the trustees and the assignees was not settled until 1861.

After 1846, the Rational Society maintained only a ghostly existence, and by 1850 its total income was only £2 5s 3d. Owen gradually lost his grip on reality, yet remained full of hope to the end, bequeathing a rich legacy of social idealism to his followers. His last three lectures were entitled 'Social Science', 'The Origin of Evil', and 'To Commence Practical Measures'.

5 Secularism

ATHEISM

The question whether lecturers should take the oath of a preacher had split the Socialist movement in 1841. Although the rebels continued to support the Rational Society and to lecture in its branches, they also commenced their own movement to agitate in the tradition of Carlile. The break was precipitated by Charles Southwell (1812–60), the social missionary in Bristol, who, as a young man, had entered the radical movement by opening a radical bookshop in Westminster in the 1830s. He had also lectured on antireligious topics on Kennington Common, and this had brought him to the notice of the Lambeth Branch of the Rational Society. Southwell was a man of action. He had fought as a volunteer in Spain as a liberal in the Carlist wars, and he loved a fight. Robert Owen was, he considered, a woolly-headed dreamer, and Southwell was one of the few Owenites who dared tell him so. The subserviency of the Central Board to the capitalists, and its hypocritical attitude towards religion, infuriated him. With the help of William Chilton (1815–55), a Bristol compositor, he commenced a new periodical, the *Oracle of Reason* (November 1841), in which he fearlessly denounced all religion as superstition and proclaimed the rational truths of atheism. In the fourth issue he wrote an article on the Bible, entitled the 'Jew Book' [**doc. 19**], and was arrested for blasphemous libel, tried at the Quarter Sessions, and sentenced to a year in Bristol gaol with a fine of £100 in addition.

This prosecution started a chain reaction of further prosecutions. Maltus Ryall (*c.* 1811–46), a member of the Lambeth branch, and George Jacob Holyoake (1817–1906) (**85, 125**), the Socialist lecturer in Sheffield, founded an Anti-Persecution Union, and took over the *Oracle*. Holyoake projected a scheme for setting up 'anti-superstitionist classes' in the Socialist branches, but it came to nothing. Men like Henry Jeffery of Edinburgh did not believe that attacks on religion could be separated from the general progress of the Social System. Holyoake found this to be only too true when, in May

1842, he delivered a lecture at Cheltenham on Home Colonisation. He scrupulously avoided all reference to God in the lecture, but at the end, a local preacher in the audience asked what place was assigned to God in a Socialist community. Holyoake's answer was embittered by the treatment accorded to Southwell, and he replied that the people were too poor to have a God, unless, like the soldiers after the late war, He were put on half-pay. This meant no more than that the incomes of the clergy should be cut, but Holyoake was arrested on the Common Law charge of blasphemy, tried at the Assizes and sentenced to six months in Gloucester gaol (**114, 153**).

Southwell's actions had not been popular. He was a rough man who did not easily endear himself to those who disagreed with him, but Holyoake had an entirely different character. Radicals of all shades of opinion came to his aid. J. A. Roebuck asked questions in the House of Commons; W. J. Fox, who had preached a sermon on behalf of Carlile in 1817, did the same for Holyoake in 1842; and Carlile himself re-entered the fray. When Holyoake went to London on bail to prepare himself for his trial, Carlile welcomed him like a long-lost son. He gave advice on how Holyoake should conduct himself, stayed at his side during the nine and a half hours of defence which Holyoake offered, and wrote letters of sympathy to Gloucester gaol instructing him on how to look after himself during his imprisonment. He also wrote to Sir Robert Peel and addressed public meetings to convince people of his opinion that Holyoake really was a Christian after all. But Holyoake was not. Like Owen he was a deist, and his treatment in prison turned him into an atheist.

The early 1840s were in many ways reminiscent of the 1820s. The spread of infidel Socialism had produced a crop of blasphemous literature of which the *Oracle* was only one example. Hetherington edited *The Freethinker's Information for the People*, in which he reprinted articles on geology, zoology and comparative religion. Reprints were also issued of Godwin's *Political Justice* and Voltaire's *Philosophical Dictionary*, and Holyoake asked for a copy of the latter to be brought to him in Gloucester gaol. For the first time, the radical theology of Germany began to appear in popular form with the publication in parts of D. F. Strauss's revolutionary *Life of Jesus* (1835; translated by George Eliot, 1846). In Manchester, a periodical entitled *The Natural Mirror, or Free Thoughts on Theology*, edited by 'an Owenian', contained extracts from, among others, Annet, Voltaire and Paine. Watson reissued copies of Volney's *Law of Nature* and Voltaire's *An Important Examination of the Holy Scriptures*. These years also resembled the 1820s in the methods adopted by the freethinkers and in the response of the authorities.

With Southwell and Holyoake in prison, the leadership of the agitation passed to Thomas Paterson, a man temperamentally similar to Southwell but who had been Holyoake's assistant in Sheffield. Ryall had taken a shop in Holywell Street as an office for the *Oracle*, and here Paterson began his campaign by displaying in the shop window a notice appropriate to the season of Christmas, 1842: 'The Existence of CHRIST alias the Baby God disproved'. He was charged with displaying obscene literature in a public thorough-fare and was imprisoned for a month. The following year a much more serious situation developed in Edinburgh. Two booksellers, Thomas Finlay (an old disciple of Carlile) and his son-in-law, Henry Robinson (who had sold unstamped newspapers in Derby, assisted by G. J. Harney), were charged with selling blasphemous and obscene literature. The Anti-Persecution Union came to their aid, and Southwell and Paterson, both newly released from gaol, hastened north to help. When the Procurator Fiscal seemed inclined not to press charges, the two Englishmen decided to keep the agitation warm. Paterson opened a 'Blasphemy Depôt' which did a fine trade selling books to the Procurator Fiscal's agents. He defied the law, abused bail, and treated the courts with contempt. Even Southwell felt that he had gone too far. Inevitably, the courts began to take their toll. Paterson received fifteen months' felon's treatment, Robinson a year in gaol and Finlay sixty days. Henry Jeffery was bound over to keep the peace and Southwell returned to England, but new volunteers kept the Blasphemy Depôt open and a young Englishwoman, Matilda Roalfe, successfully defied the authorities (**2, 8**). As in the 1820s, the power of the courts could punish but could not silence the freethinkers.

Meanwhile, in London, a remarkable freethought movement was developing. Not only were the various Halls of Science and Social Institutions centres for freethought discussion groups and lectures, but a London Atheistical Society had been set up to agitate for a change in the law as it affected infidels, and a Free Thinkers Tract Society had been formed to disseminate radical literature. Some of the members, such as Thomas Powell, had been given their appren-ticeship in blasphemy by Carlile in the 1820s. The London Atheistical Society had many members who also supported the Anti-Persecution

Union, of which Holyoake became secretary shortly after his release from gaol in August 1843. He let the *Oracle* run on until the end of the year, and then replaced it with a more moderate periodical, the *Movement*. But with the decline of Socialism, the infidel organisations began to weaken. The Anti-Persecution Union was burdened with debt and the *Movement* also had to close. Holyoake went to Glasgow in 1845 as lecturer to the Socialist branch there, but he soon found himself redundant. The Socialists had run out of money.

The radical movement generally was at a low ebb in 1846. James Watson was alarmed. He was moving his publishing business to a new shop in Queen's Head Passage, but, he wrote to Holyoake in January, 'all the pamphlets issued against superstition or religion for years past lay on the shelves like so much waste paper', and he attributed this to 'the want of a weekly periodical devoted to theological investigation' (**2**). Holyoake was convinced, and in June 1846 he took over the last Owenite journal, the *Herald of Progress*, and combined it with a new freethought periodical called the *Reasoner*. This was to appear every week until 1861, and round it Holyoake was to build a new movement which, in 1852, he called Secularism.

HOLYOAKE AND SECULARISM

The Secularist movement was the direct heir of Socialism. It took over the ideas, buildings and membership of the old Rational Society. In 1845 Holyoake wrote a short but influential book, *Rationalism, a Treatise for the Times*, in which he aimed to rescue the basic doctrines of Owenism from the ruins of the community experiment, and to put them forward as a philosophy for individuals as well as for society [**doc. 20**]. The teaching on circumstances, free will, punishment, and education which the Secularist lecturers offered to their audiences, is to be found in Owen's *Book of the New Moral World* which was the textbook of the Socialist lecturers. When Southwell returned to London in 1844 he based his operations on the Charlotte Street Institute, which had been a centre of Socialism since 1830. The John Street Social Institute remained the metropolitan centre for all ultra-radical movements. The City Road Hall of Science became the traditional home of London Secularism. In Stockport and Sheffield the local Socialists kept their Halls of Science open and when Holyoake started the Secularist movement, they simply transferred their allegiance. In Leicester and Northampton, the same men were leaders of Secularism in the 1860s as had led the Socialists twenty years earlier. The two most prominent men in the early Secularist movement, Holyoake and Robert Cooper, were both lifelong Socialists. Cooper, whose elder brother kept a radical bookshop in Manchester, had been educated in the school of the Salford Social Institution. His lectures on the Holy Scriptures had been mentioned by the Bishop of Exeter in the House of Lords in 1840. He continued as a Socialist lecturer throughout the 1840s and was still offering his services in the 1850s. The continuity from Socialism to Secularism is particularly marked in Manchester. When the Hall of Science closed down, Southwell led a revival in 1849 and reopened it. When it closed again the following year, and a smaller Social Institution was acquired, an address from Robert Owen was read at the opening, and when Cooper lectured there in 1852 he recognised many old faces in the audience. This Social Institution became a Secular Institution by changing nothing except its name.

Between 1846 and 1849 Holyoake was unable to halt the decline of Socialism. The circulation of the *Reasoner* fell to below a thousand. Emigration thinned the radical ranks, and the economic depression of 1847 may have cut short the lives of many decaying and bankrupt societies. Chartism revived and attracted some former Socialist supporters. The Society of Theological Utilitarians, as Holyoake had grandly called his new organisation, was a failure, but after the collapse of Chartism, the Socialist cause revived. Holyoake therefore changed his emphasis and in 1852 announced a new Central Secular Society.

Secularism did not attack Christianity as such. Its sphere of controversy was 'the criticism of Sacred Books and existing Religions only in those respects in which they seem to contradict ascertained Moral Truths, and are impediments to Rational progress'. Previously, the atheists had argued that a philosophy of the unknowable was meaningless and a root cause of human ignorance, error and misery. Now, Holyoake was prepared to treat religion as an irrelevant speculation and was even prepared to co-operate with Christians in promoting the secular good [**doc. 21**].

This sounded remarkably like Owen's version of Socialism, and it inherited many of Socialism's enemies. A Congregationalist minister, the Reverend Brewin Grant, who had been one of the clergymen to attack Socialism in 1840, launched a new mission against the infidels. As in 1840, the opposition merely served to advertise the opponents of Christianity and to increase their numbers. Grant twice challenged Holyoake to public debate on the relative merits of Christianity and Secularism—in London for six nights early in 1853, and in Glasgow for six nights in October 1854. Between these two debates, Secularism reached a new peak, and Holyoake was the undoubted leader of the new movement. The circulation of the *Reasoner* reached five thousand, and nearly forty local societies were reported in its pages. Secularism became a topic of conversation. It was denounced from the pulpits, discussed in the press, and declaimed against from the platform. Horace Mann used the new word to describe the unconscious creed of the lower classes (**39**). The conscious membership was probably no more than four thousand, but with many more adherents.

Meanwhile Holyoake had been encouraged to organise a national movement. His Central Secular Society became the London Secular Society, with James Watson as its first president, but the time was not ripe for a large organisation. The best way to link the local societies was through the press. Henry Hetherington had died in the cholera outbreak of 1849 and his business had been amalgamated with that of James Watson. In 1853 Holyoake took over Watson's stock and opened his own Fleet Street House. He made this place a centre for radical movements, both British and foreign, as well as a business in which a whole generation of ultra-radical printers and publishers learned their trade, but Holyoake could not handle money, and the place sank deeper and deeper into debt. As the business absorbed more and more of his time, he began to lose touch with the movement he was supposed to be leading. The ordinary membership, mainly in the North, comprised factory workers, artisans, tradesmen, shopkeepers and the like, but in London, Holyoake was making friends and depending upon wealthy patrons such as W. H. Ashurst (Owen's lawyer) and W. J. Birch, an Oxfordshire magistrate. His abilities as a journalist were bringing him to the notice of John Stuart Mill, G. H. Lewes and F. W. Newman, which enabled him to add to Secularism the finer sensibilities of the 'Victorian doubters', but his efforts were not always supported in the back-street halls. Local provincial leaders felt that Holyoake had departed too far from the true infidel tradition. 'Oh, for an hour of such critics of clerical men and things as Thomas Paine', sighed

J. H. McGuire of Glasgow in 1854. 'Oh, for such a leader for a week as Richard Carlile' (*Investigator*, 1854) (**10**).

The real strength of Secularism lay in the old Owenite areas of Lancashire and the West Riding. Although the first attempts at national organisation had failed, provincial organisations flourished among the inhabitants of Stalybridge and Stockport, Huddersfield and Halifax, Leeds and Manchester. A West Riding Secular Alliance was formed in 1852, which set the pace not only for Lancashire, but also for Glasgow and Birmingham. Methodist-style circuits were arranged to link the villages to nearby towns. Joint camp meetings were held in Shipley Glen, or high in the Pennines at Saltersbrook. Memories of Socialism and Chartism inspired Secularism to become a mass movement for social and political reform. 'Is it forgotten how many have met at Blackstone-Edge, at Skircoat Moor, or at Shipley Glen?' the editor of the *Yorkshire Tribune* asked his readers in 1855. 'It will be so again when we give the call.'

These mass meetings reached a climax in 1860, but before that, between 1857 and 1859, Holyoake's influence had begun to wane. Robert Cooper was more influential in his native North than was Holyoake, and Cooper objected to Holyoake's abandonment of outright atheism. Holyoake had, in fact, become what was later known as an 'agnostic'. So Cooper started a new journal, the *Investigator*, in 1854, which was to propagate atheistic Secularism. Around this paper developed an anti-Holyoake group. Holyoake could probably have weathered the storm if he had been successful, but he was not. As faithful Secularists poured their sixpences into the seemingly bottomless abyss of the Fleet Street House, they began to fear another Harmony Hall fiasco. Holyoake was also developing other interests, and in 1859 was tired and ill. By the end of the 1850s he seems to have opted out of the Secularist leadership, and the first stage in the development of Secularism was over (**119, 129, 131**).

BRADLAUGH AND SECULARISM

In these circumstances Charles Bradlaugh came on the scene. He had been born in Hoxton, North London, in 1833, was a religious youth, and became a Sunday school teacher at St Peter's, Hackney Road, until he was suspended after asking the incumbent, the Reverend

J. G. Packer, about discrepancies in the Thirty-Nine Articles. Instead of attending church, therefore, he spent his Sundays in Victoria Park, listening to the freethought lecturers there, and in 1849 he left home for lodgings at the Warner Street Temperance Hall where Mrs Eliza Sharples-Carlile was caretaker. Bradlaugh's new views lost him his job and he was desperately in debt, so he joined the army and went to Ireland. In 1853 a legacy enabled him to buy himself out, and he took a job as an attorney's clerk. To avoid damaging his employer's reputation, he adopted the pseudonym 'Iconoclast' (the image-breaker) at this time, and used it till 1868. He remained with various legal firms till 1870, thereby gaining invaluable experience in the law, but from 1858 lecturing was increasingly occupying his time (**123**).

Bradlaugh was a naturally brilliant orator, and his mind was as alert as his style was vigorous. He shared Robert Cooper's dislike of Holyoake's cautious avoidance of the word 'atheist' because, for him, religion was an inevitable stumbling block in the way of progress and could not simply be ignored. Holyoake had developed Secularism because he appreciated the changes which were taking place in public opinion and he wished, by moderation, to attract as wide a base of support as possible. Bradlaugh, in contrast, wanted open warfare. His tactics met with opposition, and opposition, as ever, contributed to the strengthening of the movement.

Secularism in the North had, like most radical movements following the Crimean War, suffered a serious decline, but after 1858 Bradlaugh set about reconstructing the branches in his own image. Without a sound basis in local organisations, the mass meetings were, to him, mere froth. Bradlaugh lectured and revival followed in his wake—in Lancashire and Yorkshire, in the north-east and Scotland, in the Midlands and London, and even in Plymouth and Great Yarmouth. The opposition which had formed round Cooper's *Investigator* accepted Bradlaugh as its leader.

The first society which Bradlaugh reformed in the North was that at Sheffield, and in 1860 this society projected a new provincial newspaper, to be called the *National Reformer*, and launched a limited company to put it on a sound financial basis. The editors were Bradlaugh and Joseph Barker who had been a Methodist and a Chartist in the 1840s, but who was a freethinker for most of the 1850s. The popularity of both men in the West Riding ensured the paper's success, and its circulation rose to five thousand. Barker, however, could not accept Bradlaugh's advocacy of birth control and radical political reform, so the two split up, and Holyoake, who had concluded his *Reasoner* in June 1861, was brought in as Bradlaugh's new partner at the beginning of 1862. The Secularists prepared to create a new national organisation to be called the National Secular Society.

Almost predictably, the Holyoake–Bradlaugh partnership did not last long, and the *National Reformer* Company was wound up. The paper became Bradlaugh's personal property and he transferred its offices to London. Between 1863 and 1866, Bradlaugh was ill, and still had to earn his living, so the paper was edited by John Watts, assisted by his brother Charles. Bradlaugh remained a frequent contributor to the *National Reformer* which, in 1866, announced a new attempt to form a national freethought organisation, 'having its headquarters and office-bearers either in London or Lancashire, and having branches in all the provincial towns' (**11**). London was decided on, and Bradlaugh was elected president with Charles Watts as his secretary. This time the organisation was successful (**119**).

The story of the National Secular Society between 1866 and 1890 is largely the story of Bradlaugh's career. This was resented by the other leaders, but Bradlaugh's ability, skill and success kept him supreme. Holyoake gave up the Fleet Street House in 1862, and the printing side of the business was continued by his brother Austin, as 'Austin & Co.' When Austin Holyoake died in 1874, his business was acquired by the National Secular Society for Charles Watts. Only once was Bradlaugh's leadership seriously challenged. In 1876 G. W. Foote left Bradlaugh and joined Holyoake in producing one of Holyoake's many but ephemeral literary efforts, the *Secularist*. Foote (1850–1915) was a man of great ability, who eventually succeeded Bradlaugh on his retirement from the National Secular Society presidency in 1890, but in 1876 he was probably jealous of Bradlaugh's dominance and the favour the latter was showing to a comparative newcomer, Mrs Annie Besant (1847–1933) (**127**).

Mrs Besant, the wife of a clergyman, had begun to lose her Christian faith about 1872, and on leaving home she came under the protection and influence of Thomas Scott, a radical freethought publisher. Scott thought Mrs Besant a very ambitious woman, which she was, but she was also a very able one. In 1874 she met Bradlaugh, was appointed a political correspondent for the *National Reformer* and joined the National Secular Society. In 1877 she and Bradlaugh became involved in a prosecution concerning the controversial birth control pamphlet, *The Fruits of Philosophy*, by Dr Charles Knowlton. James Watson had first published the pamphlet in England in 1832, and the work had passed with the business to the Holyoakes and then to Charles Watts who acquired the original plates after Watson's death in 1874. Two years later, the pamphlet was the subject of a prosecution in Bristol. Watts acknowledged himself to be the publisher, but thought the work indefensible and so pleaded guilty. Bradlaugh had been an active spokesman for 'neo-Malthusian' principles for twenty years, and so he and Mrs Besant decided to reissue the Knowlton pamphlet. Watts immediately joined Foote and Holyoake in opposition and they started the British Secular Union to rival the National Secular Society. Bradlaugh and Besant were prosecuted and found guilty, but the decision was reversed on appeal. The British Secular Union was successful at first, but did not last long, Foote soon rejoining Bradlaugh and starting his own paper, the *Freethinker*, in 1881. Watts emigrated to Canada in 1884 and did not return until after Bradlaugh's death. Holyoake pursued his own increasingly eccentric course, more as a radical journalist than as a Secularist. The printing business was continued by Watts's son, Charles Albert, but Bradlaugh and Besant also started their own Freethought Publishing Company.

The early 1880s were dominated by Bradlaugh's attempt to enter Parliament, when his public reputation was at its highest. Radicals of all opinions supported him, and the *National Reformer* became more than a freethought journal—it was recognised as the national organ of the ultra-radical cause. The National Secular Society benefited from its association with Bradlaugh's name, membership figures reaching a new peak of six thousand in 1880. The best year was 1885, when there were over a hundred branches throughout the country. In addition to the members, there were many more adherents. At Leicester, for example, Bradlaugh addressed a meeting at which over three thousand persons were said to be present, and in London there were at least twenty places at which outdoor meetings were regularly held. This was the climax. After 1885 a slow decline set in and the National Secular Society never regained its losses. Bradlaugh entered Parliament and was no longer able to give Secularism his undivided attention at a time when he was needed to maintain his following in the face of increased rivalry from the new Socialist movement. In 1890 there were only sixty-two branches of the

National Secular Society. 'The heroic period of Freethought is well-nigh over', warned Foote in 1890 when he became president of the Society (**119**).

Bradlaugh was suffering from Bright's disease and died in 1891. Two years later, the *National Reformer* closed and Mrs Besant left the Secularists and Socialists to join the Theosophists. On the credit side, Charles Watts returned from Canada, and Foote conducted his *Freethinker* and the National Secular Society in its post-heroic stage with considerable success. 'Wherever I go,' wrote the Reverend Hugh Price Hughes to Holyoake, 'I find some of Mr Foote's followers distributing pamphlets' (**2**). Holyoake himself was back in the pamphlet business in 1890, but on a more respectable and sophisticated level. In that year he helped form the Propaganda Press Committee, which in 1899 became the Rationalist Press Association. The printer for the Association was Charles Albert Watts, direct heir to the business of Charles Watts, the Holyoake brothers, James Watson and Henry Hetherington (**122**). However, in 1900 the National Secular Society no longer had any hope of commanding a mass movement. The promise of the 1850s and 1880s was not to be fulfilled.

6 Liberalism, Chartism and Republicanism

LIBERALISM

No single working-class movement was predominant in the years between the failure of Owenism and Chartism in the 1840s and the rise of Socialism in the 1880s, but Secularism contained within itself many of the features of the various reform organisations of these years. The work of the Secularists illustrates the part played by the infidel-radical tradition of Paine, Carlile and Owen in mid-Victorian politics and society.

The attitude of the Secularists to society is best outlined in John Stuart Mill's famous *Essay on Liberty*, published in 1859. Freedom was to be the key word of their philosophy—freedom from government interference and public opinion; freedom from all restrictions on the expression of ideas. This liberal attitude meant that Secularists involved themselves in a large number and variety of reform movements, either as individuals or collectively. Many of them were temperance or total abstinence advocates; some were vegetarians and antivivisectionists, most were advocates of women's rights; and some pioneered the spread of knowledge about birth control. Above all, Secularists demanded national secular education, the abolition of church rates and tithes, and the repeal of Sabbatarian legislation. They advocated full civil rights for all citizens, and wished for complete freedom to express all their demands in public.

The education issue was fundamental to the rationalist's interpretation of life. Paine's famous phrase rang down the decades: 'One good schoolmaster is of more use than a hundred priests.' Education was central to the Owenite concept of the new moral world, and the Secularists continued this tradition. Sunday schools were attached to practically every Social Institution, Secular Hall and Hall of Science, and many of these had day schools as well. Holyoake supported Richard Cobden's National Public School Association in 1850, and Joseph Chamberlain's National Education League twenty years later. The Secularists were opposed to the Education Acts of 1870 and 1902, which allowed public money to be spent on sectarian education, and the demand for completely secular public education is still, today, a major item in the National Secular Society's programme (**119**).

The freedom of the press was essential for the education of the public, and the agitation for the removal of the laws which imposed legal and financial restrictions on newspapers was one of the most constant themes of nineteenth-century radical history. In 1836 the Stamp Duty stood at a penny on newspapers; advertisements and paper were still liable for duty; and a securities system meant that printers and publishers had to provide considerable sureties against committing blasphemous, seditious and obscene libels. The Secularists, in alliance with other radical groups, began a systematic campaign against these laws in the 1850s. A Newspaper Stamp Abolition Committee was created in 1849, at the suggestion of Francis Place, out of the remnants of one of the Chartist groups, the People's Charter Union, and in 1851 this body became the Association for the Repeal of the Taxes on Knowledge (1851–70). Freethinkers were among its most active members, and Holyoake used his *Reasoner* to collect hundreds of sixpences for the campaign fund. The main object of attack was the Blasphemous and Seditious Libels Act of 1819 [**doc. 9**], as modified by the Stamp Act of 1836, and the policy of the Association was to reveal the absurdities of the law by forcing cases against the respectable press and obtaining precise definitions of the law from the judges (**113**).

The outbreak of the Crimean War in 1854 proved to be the turning-point in the Association's campaign, as the demand for news of the war made any restrictions on the press seem irksome to all publishers. Sensing the growing public support for the Association's objects, Holyoake issued a weekly unstamped *War Fly Sheet* (13 December 1854 to 22 June 1855) in contravention of the law. For doing this he received a number of summonses from the Exchequer Court, and was fined a total of over £600,000, none of which he paid. The law was clearly unenforceable, and in June 1855 the stamp was made optional.

The radical agitators were greatly helped by Gladstone. In 1853, as Chancellor of the Exchequer, he had accepted a radical motion abolishing the Advertisement Duty, and in 1860, as part of the Cobden Commercial Treaty with France, he agreed to abolish the Paper Duty. This the House of Lords refused to accept, so Gladstone incorporated the measure in the 1861 Budget, which, traditionally, the Lords could not amend. All that now remained of the oppressive legislation erected against the press during and after the Napoleonic Wars was the system of securities. As the registering of papers had been done with the stamp, before 1855 the unstamped press had often managed to avoid the need to be registered, but after the abolition of the stamp, the government enforced the law more strictly. Holyoake again began a provocative campaign, but the Stamp Office refused to be drawn, and an uneasy truce was maintained between Fleet Street and the government until the Inland Revenue Board appointed a new solicitor in 1866. He commenced a new series of prosecutions against unregistered papers, and one of his chosen victims was Charles Bradlaugh's *National Reformer*. Bradlaugh contested the case, but before a decision had been reached, Gladstone became Prime Minister (1868), and he appointed as Secretary to the Treasury A. S. Ayrton, one of the principal campaigners against the Taxes on Knowledge. So, in 1869, the last financial restrictions on the press were removed (**113**).

This still left the legal restrictions on freedom of expression and publication, but the blasphemy laws were gradually relaxed during the course of the nineteenth century. In 1857 a Cornish well-digger, Thomas Pooley, was convicted for scrawling 'Duloe stinks of the monster Christ's Bible—T. Pooley' on the gate of the local vicar. This conviction was thought to be the first application of the blasphemy laws in England since 1840, and, apart from being a dangerous revival, it was also a gross miscarriage of justice, as Pooley was obviously mad. Holyoake visited Cornwall, made a full 'exposure' in the press, and secured a reprieve from the Home Secretary (**2**).

The laws of libel were also used to censor the contents of books and to prevent the circulation of literature which was regarded as being seditious, obscene or blasphemous. In 1858 Edward Truelove (an Owenite who had started business as a bookseller at the John Street Institution) was prosecuted for publishing a seditious pamphlet, *Tyrannicide: is it Justifiable?* by W. E. Adams. A Press Prosecution Committee was formed, with James Watson as treasurer and Bradlaugh as secretary, and Truelove was acquitted. The next important case was over the Knowlton pamphlet in 1877. Bradlaugh and Besant were convicted of obscene libel and were each fined £200 and imprisoned for six months for republishing the offending pamphlet, but on appeal the sentences were quashed; the pamphlet continued to be sold, and Mrs Besant brought out her own *Law of Population* as well (**127**). The most important legal decision concerning blasphemous libel was obtained by G. W. Foote in 1882. He had been prosecuted for printing a series of vulgar 'Bible Sketches' in his *Freethinker* and was gaoled for a year, but when a second charge of a similar nature was brought against him, Lord Chief Justice Coleridge (who had been Pooley's prosecutor in 1857) ruled that the law was concerned with the manner, not the matter, of blasphemy, and this has been the usual interpretation of the law ever since (**119**).

The Secularists' greatest achievement was in their campaign for civil rights, especially in the matter of affirmation. In the first half of the nineteenth century the law required in the courts an oath from all witnesses. Atheists were held to be incapable of taking a meaningful oath, and were therefore treated as outlaws. Robert Owen's lecturers had frequently been discriminated against in this way, but in 1855 an Affirmations Act allowed persons with religious objections to the oath to affirm instead, and the freethinkers began a campaign to have the Act extended to include their own secular objections as well. This agitation reached a climax in 1861 when Sir J. S. Trelawney brought an Affirmations Bill before Parliament. Holyoake immediately set up an 'Evidence Committee' to produce examples of how unjust the existing law was and the whole Secularist movement was harnessed to bring pressure to bear on Parliament. A test case involving a member of the Rochdale Secular Society was lost, however, and Trelawney's Bill was defeated by four votes on the second reading. As with other measures of liberal reform, secular affirmations were not legalised until after Gladstone had come to power in 1868.

Charles Bradlaugh decided to contest the 1868 general election and offered himself as a member for Northampton. He was defeated then, and again in 1874, but was finally elected in 1880. Every M.P. was required to take an oath on entering Parliament, but Bradlaugh applied instead to make an affirmation according to the Act of 1869. Mr Speaker Brand refused this request and appointed a Select Committee to consider whether the Affirmations Act could be applied to the House of Commons. The Committee decided against Bradlaugh, who therefore offered to take the usual oath. A small group of Conservative M.P.s—the 'Fourth Party' led by Lord Randolph Churchill—objected to this on the grounds that Bradlaugh had admitted the oath to be meaningless for him, and a second committee was appointed. This time the decision was that Bradlaugh might affirm, but in so doing he would be risking prosecution for taking his seat illegally, but by a narrow majority (275–230) the House voted to keep Bradlaugh out. Bradlaugh ignored this, entered the House, refused to withdraw, and was locked in the Clock Tower for the night. Shades of 'Wilkes and Liberty' began to walk again, and public opinion moved round to support the excluded member. He was finally permitted to affirm, but a writ was issued charging him with sitting in the House illegally, and the courts decided against him.

The Conservative Opposition, inspired by the 'Fourth Party', used the Bradlaugh Case to harass Gladstone's ministry for the next four years. In 1881 Bradlaugh was re-elected by Northampton and forcibly ejected from the House. He returned, administered the oath to himself, was expelled, and again contested Northampton (1882). Again he was re-elected and the Liberal Government introduced an Affirmations Bill which was defeated by three votes (292–289). Bradlaugh decided to appeal to the courts once more, so he again administered the oath to himself and then resigned to seek a new mandate from his constituents (1884). Again they returned him, and he was elected once more at the general election of 1885. A new Speaker had been appointed at the end of 1883—Peel, the younger son of Sir Robert—and when the House met in 1885 he permitted Bradlaugh to take the oath (**124**).

A significant victory had been won, and an important step taken in the creation of the modern, liberal, and secular state, but the struggle had exhausted Bradlaugh. He did good radical work in Parliament, and successfully introduced an Affirmations Bill, but by this time he was a dying man. The original motion of 1880, excluding Bradlaugh from the House, was expunged on 27 January 1891. Three days later, Bradlaugh died.

CHARTISM

The secular societies were officially neutral in political affairs, but in fact most of the members seem to have supported the liberal-radical politics of the leadership, and to have taken up the causes of parliamentary reform at home and republicanism abroad. This was only to be expected. 'Freethought is of the nature of intellectual republicanism', wrote Holyoake. 'All are equal who think and the only distinction is in the capacity of thinking.' As in many other aspects of radicalism, Thomas Paine had set the trend when he had supported the American and French Revolutions, but Paine was also a constitutionalist, and it is a further characteristic of British radicalism that it was almost exclusively non-revolutionary. The reformers did not seek to subvert the parliamentary constitution, but to change it. Their more violent aspirations were reserved for the overthrow of foreign despots.

Chartism itself was not one movement but many. Its one unifying feature was the demand for political reform as expressed in the People's Charter (**103**). Within the Chartist ranks, sober educational-ists united with starving factory workers, and political realists with millenarian preachers. Many of the leaders were artisan-collec-tivists, like Lovett, but among the most influential were individualists with strong Tory sympathies, like Stephens and O'Connor. The same diversity was to be found in the attitudes of the Chartists towards religion (**47**). Men of all kinds of beliefs were to be found within the Chartist movement. The links between the infidel radicals and the Chartists were numerous, but their two groups remained distinct. The Owenites had a lofty contempt for 'mere' politics, and, as Charles Southwell said in 1843: 'There cannot be any useful organic change in the constitution of human society, so long as the humbler members of it remain in bondage to religion.' William Lovett was unable to share this view, so he gradually drew apart from the Owenites in the late 1830s; Henry Vincent was totally opposed to the attack on religion and regarded the infidelity of Owenism as a national evil; but other Chartists were very favourable towards the Socialists. Relations were cordial between Holyoake and G. J. Harney when they were the representatives of their respective movements in Sheffield during 1841–42, and, while Holyoake was in prison, Harney acted as the Sheffield agent for the *Oracle of Reason* and the Anti-Persecution Union. But in 1848, Harney quite correctly refused to recognise Holyoake as a Chartist and made a clear distinction between infidelity and political reform [**doc. 24**]. Only after the eclipse of O'Connor did the Secularist leaders come to play a part in the various Chartist organisations.

Most Secularists, however, advocated universal suffrage. The *Yorkshire Tribune* in 1855 set out a programme which probably reflects the interests of the ordinary members of the secular societies in the West Riding. The points of the programme were:

1. Universal suffrage
2. The rights of labour
3. Secular education by the state
4. Nationalisation of land
5. Home colonisation
6. Maine Law (i.e. total abstinence from alcoholic drinks, enforced by law)
7. Rights of women
8. Freedom of opinion.

These eight points were the major planks in the radical platform. Some were more widely held than others. For example, the Maine Law was extremely controversial, and its imposition in the United States had actually disgusted Joseph Barker with the blind power of democracy, but, generally speaking, the leaders of the working classes differed more widely over means than over ends. Their choice was whether to aim at the creation of a class-based agitation for reform, or whether to join the middle classes and compromise on principle where necessary. Holyoake, who was elected to the Executive Committee of O'Connor's National Charter Association in 1851, seemed in almost indecent haste to abandon principle, and he joined Sir Joshua Walmsley's National Parliamentary and Financial Reform Association in 1851. Southwell was more cautious, but wrote in 1849: 'Animated by a spirit superior to mere partisanship, we see good in Chartism, in Socialism, and last not least, in Financial Reform.' The Chartist leaders slowly came round to this point of view. Harney, the spokesman for the extremists, gradually moderated his policy, and even Ernest Jones, the brightest hope of Karl Marx, began to work with the middle classes in 1858 (**107, 110**).

The Crimean War divided the radical movement, and the 1857 general election practically destroyed the radical group in Parliament, but in 1858 the signs of revival appeared. By this time, Holyoake had decided to subordinate all class interests to the Liberalism of John Stuart Mill, John Bright and Gladstone, and in this context did good work. In 1858 he joined Joseph Cowen's Northern Reform Union, and acted as its London agent and Fleet Street representative. In 1860, he was a member of the London

Political Union, one of the organisations which promoted the Reform League in 1865, of which both Holyoake and Bradlaugh were members (**109**). In 1868, Holyoake's pamphlet on the ballot was issued by the Reform League, and widely circulated among M.P.s.

Holyoake was, however, more moderate in his approach than many of his followers. Not all Secularists shared his willingness to compromise on such a fundamental principle as universal suffrage, and Charles Bradlaugh was infuriated when Holyoake supported the 'intelligence franchise' as a temporary measure in 1858. It is difficult, though, to generalise about individual attitudes. Robert Cooper, for example, the most outspoken Secularist in the North, was a founder member of the Reform Union which advocated household suffrage and he defended compromise on the grounds of political realism (**4**).

REPUBLICANISM

The same conflict of principle and practice is to be found in the attitudes of the ultra-radicals to republicanism. Freethinkers were theoretical republicans, but their principles were difficult to apply in Victorian England. When Bradlaugh lectured on the Prince of Wales, for example, his subject was George, the Prince Regent, not Albert Edward, the contemporary Prince and future Edward VII. During Victoria's reign, republican feelings were strongly held only for a few years, in 1848 and in 1869–73, and the impetus on each occasion came from France.

The Secularists played a leading part in what republicanism there was, and the moderation shown by Holyoake, and even by Bradlaugh, illustrates the spirit of compromise which pervaded British radicalism in the middle decades of the nineteenth century. On 9 April 1848, on the eve of the last great Chartist meeting, Holyoake lectured to a large audience at the John Street Institution on 'The Chances of obtaining an English Republic by Moral Means'. This gave him the reputation for being a republican, but he did little to deserve it. In 1855 Harney and Joseph Cowen invited him to become a member of their Republican Brotherhood, but it was concerned mainly with foreign affairs. Bradlaugh was more extreme, but his domestic republicanism was equally impotent. After the failure of the Reform League to win seats for working-class candidates at the 1868 general election, republican feeling revived. It was aimed not only at the monarchy, though the Queen had become very unpopular after her withdrawal from public life following the death of the Prince Consort in 1861; it was aimed also at the whole structure of aristocracy and landlordism. In 1869 a Land and Labour League was founded to agitate for an English Republic on principles laid down by Karl Marx for the International Working Men's Association. Bradlaugh was an enthusiastic member. He had found the newly formed Labour Electoral League beneath his notice, and had scorned to join John Stuart Mill's Land Tenure Reform Association. (Holyoake, in contrast, was a member of both, but not of the Land and Labour League.) Instead Bradlaugh worked with the extremists, and many Secularists followed his lead. In 1873, there were about fifty republican clubs throughout the country, many of them organised by Secularists. In Birmingham, for example, the local Secularist and Co-operative leader, Christopher Charles Cattell, was also founder of the Republican Club, and when a conference of republicans was called in Birmingham in 1873, Bradlaugh was one of the organisers and G. W. Foote took the Chair. Two years earlier, Bradlaugh had put his republican views in print in his *The Impeachment of the House of Brunswick* (1871), which attacked the Royal Family, and especially the four Georges, and recommended the abolition of the monarchy on the death of the Queen [**doc. 27**].

Such republicanism was never very successful in England. Bradlaugh and George Odger, the conveners of the Republican Conference, both quarrelled with the Land and Labour League because they could not accept the extremism of the Paris Commune which the League supported, and the *Republican*, the unofficial paper of the League, attacked Bradlaugh for his atheism. The republican mood of the early 1870s passed, and by the time of the Queen's Jubilee in 1887, republicanism was virtually dead (**109**).

The ultra-radicals had more success abroad. Republicanism was an international movement: in the 1840s London was the home of the continental refugees and the English radicals were busily engaged in helping them, sharing their plans, and encouraging their ventures. Exiles from Poland, Germany, Hungary and Italy kept the republican tradition alive (**110**).

The defeat of the European revolutions of 1848 was followed by a proliferation of radical activity. Ledru-Rollin, Louis Blanc, Francis Pultsky, Joseph Mazzini, Louis Kossuth, and many others, were incorporated into the English radical scene. A Polish Refugee Fund, a Kossuth Fund and an Italian Loan Fund were established; the radical press was full of appeals, and help also came in a less open way. Thomas Allsop, a Birmingham Owenite, manufactured some bombs for the Italian patriot, Felice Orsini, and Holyoake tested a prototype while he was on one of his lecture tours (**85, 125**). When Orsini used the bombs in an attempt on the life of Napoleon III in 1857 Palmerston introduced a Conspiracy Bill, to give the government greater powers to deal with the refugees. Holyoake, Ashurst (son of Owen's lawyer who had died in 1855), James Stansfeld (brother-in-law of Ashurst and a future radical M.P.) and William Shaen, M.P., formed an Anti-Conspiracy Bill Committee at 147 Fleet Street, and organised a demonstration in Hyde Park. At the same time, the radicals in Parliament, led by Milner-Gibson (President of the Association for the Repeal of the Taxes on Knowledge), forced the defeat of the Bill on the second reading, and the resignation of Palmerston's government.

The major republican issue at the end of the 1850s was Italy. As early as 1856, Holyoake had printed in the *Reasoner* an appeal for money to buy a thousand rifles for the first Italian province to rise, and in 1860 all efforts were concentrated on raising money to send a volunteer British Legion to fight alongside Garibaldi. Holyoake was acting secretary to the Garibaldi Committee, and also a member of the subcommittee which arranged the dispatch of the Legion. Austin Holyoake assisted with recruiting, and Charles Bradlaugh lectured in support of Italian liberation (**3**). The Secularists were drawn into the republican movement for theological as well as secular reasons. The Italian struggle was seen as the fight of Garibaldi, the atheist, against the power of the Pope. The republican campaign was directed against the Holy Alliance of Catholic Powers, against which the French and every subsequent revolution was regarded as having been fought.

Bradlaugh visited Italy in 1861. Ten years later he went to Paris in an unsuccessful attempt to negotiate between Thiers and the Commune, and in 1873 he went to Spain on behalf of the English republicans to congratulate Castellar, the successful republican leader (**123**). Ireland, however, was Bradlaugh's main interest. In 1867 he attained notoriety for his defence of the Irish Fenians, and he helped draft their manifesto, though he did not share all their views. In 1868 he wrote a pamphlet on the Irish question, and received support from the Irish Land League in his attempt to win the Northampton election in the same year. The land question linked the English and Irish radicals, and the president of the Land and Labour League was Patrick Hennessey, an Irishman. Although the Catholic Irish opposed Bradlaugh's entry into Parliament in 1880, after 1885 Bradlaugh was an outspoken supporter of Irish interests in Parliament.

Towards the end of his life, he gave equal support to India. The East had always had an appeal to freethinkers, and Bradlaugh became known as 'the Member for India'. He visited India shortly before his death, and at his funeral, Gandhi was one of the mourners. The closest link of all between Secularism and India, however, was that provided by Mrs Besant. Through Theosophy, she became familiar with Indian ways of thought, and in her later years she was a president of the Indian National Congress. These interests had already been foreshadowed in her Secularist career: as early as 1879 she was writing about the problems of India and Afghanistan (**127**).

These were the policies of British freethought in the mid-nineteenth century. Secularism was a culmination of the old radical infidel tradition, and in its organisation and membership it epitomised mid-Victorian working-class radicalism. Yet Secularism was only one side of the working-class movement. How much of its legacy was in fact passed on to the modern labour movement of the twentieth century? In many ways, the old tradition of Thomas Paine comes to an end with the decline of the Secularists and the things for which they stood. The British Labour movement rested on not one foundation, but many.

Part Three

CONCLUSION

7 Socialism

THE LABOUR MOVEMENT

Following the failure of the Reform League to compel the Liberal Party to secure seats for some working-class representatives of labour in Parliament, a Labour Representation League was set up in September 1869, but it remained securely under the control of the moderates and the Liberal Party. Its successes were few, and at the 1874 election, only two working men, both of them miners, were sent to Westminster. Gladstone's first ministry (1868–74) had carried out many useful reforms, but it had proved a great disappointment to the radicals. The 1870 Education Act continued the practice of giving state funds to religious bodies, and, above all, the Liberals had shirked the labour issue. The trade unions were given legal status in 1871, but a new Criminal Law Amendment Act was passed which made even peaceful picketing illegal. The government seemed to be taking away with one hand what it had just given with the other, and in this crisis, the leaders of the great amalgamated unions (the 'Junta') followed the examples of the Manchester and Birmingham Trades Councils in 1868 and 1869 respectively, and called a Trades Union Congress in 1871. The T.U.C. could not prevent the Criminal Law Amendment Act from being brought into force, and so it mounted an agitation for repeal, and appointed a Parliamentary Committee to watch over the interests of labour in Parliament (**24, 109**).

The Labour Representation League and the Parliamentary Committee of the T.U.C. were hardly the beginnings of a modern labour movement in Parliament. The former body was content with promoting 'Lib-Labism' and the latter was concerned solely with trade union matters. The real labour movement at this time existed in the radical clubs, dominated by men like Charles Bradlaugh, and in the 1880s these clubs blossomed out in a Socialist revival. In March 1881, a conference was called at the headquarters of the German Social Democrats in London, to form a democratic party completely distinct from the Liberal Party. This move was supported by Joseph

Cowen, the radical M.P. for Newcastle upon Tyne who had led radical republicanism in the north-east for over thirty years. As a result of the conference, a Democratic Federation was set up to rival Joseph Chamberlain's National Liberal Federation. H. M. Hyndman, a 'Tory' radical who had fallen under the influence of Karl Marx, gradually came to dominate the new Federation, and in 1884 he turned it into a Marxist organisation called the Social Democratic Federation (S.D.F.). As the old Liberal members moved out, so new Socialists were brought in, among them H. H. Champion (the secretary) and William Morris. The Socialist leaders differed in outlook and approach, but the S.D.F. slowly grew, helped by the onset of an economic recession in 1886. On 8 February in that year, a meeting was organised in Trafalgar Square to demand public works for the unemployed. Champion and John Burns made fiery speeches and the crowd got out of hand. The police then moved the meeting on to Hyde Park, but windows of clubs in Pall Mall were smashed *en route*. Socialism suddenly achieved national publicity, alarming the rich and respectable, but in fact the S.D.F. probably had no more than a thousand members.

The S.D.F. was the first Socialist group, but not the only one. Others included William Morris's Socialist League and, more important, the Fabian Society. The first Fabians included Frank Podmore (the biographer of Robert Owen), Edward Pease, George Bernard Shaw, and Hubert Bland, and they were soon joined by Sidney Webb and Mrs Annie Besant. Most of the members were brought to Socialism by Henry George, an American, whose *Progress and Poverty* (1880) advocated a single land tax, and their Socialism belonged to the drawing-room until Mrs Besant brought to them her ten years' experience in the radical clubs of London. In November 1887 she helped organise a mammoth march to protest at the closing of Trafalgar Square by the police after a series of weekend labour riots, and when two speakers in the square, John Burns and Cunninghame Graham, M.P., were arrested, she started a Law and Liberty League. Her most notable contribution to the Labour movement, though, came in 1888 when, as a result of an article in the *Link* (the journal of the Law and Liberty League), which described the conditions of work in the lucifer match factories, over six hundred match-girls came out on strike. Mrs Besant and Herbert Burrows organised a strike fund, and the girls won concessions from their employers. Also in 1888, Mrs Besant contested a seat on the London

School Board and was elected to represent Tower Hamlets. The Fabians as a group entered London politics the following year when the London County Council was set up, though, true to their name, they adopted the policy of permeating the Liberals by joining them in a Progressive Party (**127, 138, 140**).

All the efforts of labour seemed doomed to end in compromise. The extreme Socialists were not sufficiently popular with the radicals, and the radicals were not sufficiently distinct from the Liberals for a separate party of labour to be set up. The Conservatives had removed the principal barrier to trade union co-operation with the Liberals when, in 1875, Disraeli's ministry legalised peaceful picketing. The S.D.F. split when H. H. Champion left Hyndman and started advocating the policy of extracting pledges on labour issues from candidates at elections, and of threatening to put up independent labour candidates where the necessary pledges were withheld. This policy was especially necessary in the provinces where wealthy industrialists could dominate the local branches of the National Liberal Federation. In 1889 a radical Scottish miner, J. Keir Hardie, contested a by-election in mid-Lanark with Champion's help. He was not successful, but a new step in labour politics had been taken, and Hardie began a Scottish Labour Party while Champion organised a National Labour Party. Meanwhile in Manchester Robert Blatchford, a journalist, had been converted to Socialism, and in 1891 he started a Socialist paper, the *Clarion*, which was astonishingly successful. Extracts from the paper by Blatchford, entitled *Merrie England*, sold hundreds of thousands of copies.

These individual efforts were brought together to form an independent labour party following political developments in Bradford. In 1889–90, the Socialist trade unionists, Will Thorne and Pete Curran, had visited Bradford and established a branch of their Gasworkers and General Labourers Union there. The *Yorkshire Factory Times*, edited by Joseph Burgess, was started to advocate labour representation, and a Bradford Labour Union was formed in 1890. Socialism and Labour Unions then spread rapidly in the West Riding as economic recession set in, and also in 1890 the Fabians made a successful tour of the same region. In 1892 a Fabian conference came out in favour of an independent labour representation in Parliament, and, in the same year, a preliminary conference was held when the annual T.U.C. meeting brought labour leaders together in Glasgow. Bradford then provided the initiative and the

desired party, called simply the Independent Labour Party (I.L.P.),
was born there in January 1893 (**138**).

This was an important development, but the labour movement
remained politically very weak. In the 1892 election only Hardie
(West Ham) and Burns (Battersea) had been elected as independent
labour members. Most of the other working-class M.P.s (eleven in
1886) were Lib-Labs, and by 1895, when Hardie lost his seat, Burns
too was moving towards Liberalism. The T.U.C. was predominantly
non-Socialist, but the legal position of the unions, thought to have
been safeguarded by the 1875 Act, was again threatened by the
courts as employers became more militant. In 1899, the T.U.C.
agreed to support a conference to discuss a new attempt to secure
representation for labour in Parliament. A Labour Electoral Committee had been set up in 1886 (renamed the Labour Electoral
Association in 1887) to replace the defunct Labour Representation
League, but, like the latter, it had succumbed to Lib-Labism. The
new conference was held in February 1900, and, almost unnoticed
by the press, the Labour Representation Committee was formed with
James Ramsay MacDonald as its first secretary. This body gradually
won the support of the unions, and at the general election in 1906
twenty-nine members were elected. The Labour Party was born
(**138**).

SECULARISM AND SOCIALISM

The infidel radical tradition had, in the Secularist movement,
become identified with Liberalism. This was to be a stumbling block,
and the Secularists did not contribute to Socialism in the same direct
way as the Owenites had contributed to Secularism. Holyoake, the
founder, Bradlaugh, the first president of the National Secular
Society, and Foote, his successor (1890–1915), were all individualists
(**119**). The foremost Secularist of the early twentieth century, J. M.
Robertson, was parliamentary secretary to the Board of Trade in
Asquith's last Liberal ministry (1911–15). Yet, despite the pronounced Liberalism of the Secularist leadership, Socialism had much
to commend it to the Secularists, who were traditional advocates of
labour representation in Parliament, and as radicals, favoured land
reform—even land nationalisation. The big division in radical policy
came between those who attacked the landlords but accepted the

76

private enterprise capitalism of the middle classes, and those who did not bother to distinguish between industrial capitalism and landlordism (**109**). A new generation of Secularists was growing up during the years of economic uncertainty as industrial capitalism was increasing in scale and remoteness, who were not so confident as the old leaders that individualism and self-help were quite the virtues they had been in mid-Victorian England (**108**). Secularism passed into Socialism despite the contrary political opinions of Charles Bradlaugh (**140**).

The National Secular Society reached its peak in the early 1880s. In April 1884 Bradlaugh met Hyndman to debate 'Will Socialism benefit the English People?' [**docs. 29, 30**]. This was the turning-point, for it set in train miniature discussions of the same kind throughout the Secularist branches. Some members, such as Jack Fitzgerald, an Irishman living in London, moved from Secularism to Socialism as a direct consequence of the debate (**36**). Others, such as Harry Snell, secretary of the Nottingham Secular Society, became Socialists after reading the printed version of the debate, though Snell did not resign from the National Secular Society till 1895 (**135**). One of the most vigorous London converts was John Burns, who was a regular speaker at radical and Secularist meetings in Battersea. In 1884 he joined the S.D.F. and shortly after the Bradlaugh–Hyndman debate, he spoke at the Battersea Secular Society on 'Poverty, its Cause and Cure'. One young man in the audience, Tom Mann, became a Socialist, and when Burns formed the Battersea branch of the S.D.F. shortly afterwards, Mann joined (**147**). Secularist branches throughout the country opened their doors to Socialist lecturers, and in so doing lost members to the new enthusiasm: the Fabians, for example, lectured in the Leicester Secular Hall; Hyndman spoke there shortly afterwards; and Morris first delivered his lecture on 'Art and Socialism' in the same hall. Snell invited Morris to speak to the Nottingham Secularists, and in Huddersfield, a branch of the Fabians was started at Thornton's Temperance Hotel, the traditional home of freethought in the town.

In theory, Secularism was not opposed to Socialism. G. W. Foote declared in 1890 that he was of no party at all, and F. J. Gould stressed the same about the Leicester Secular Society (**121**). The hostility of Hyndman, Blatchford and other Socialist leaders to the Christian Church helped men to feel at home in both movements but divided loyalties proved a strain for men with limited time and money. Generally speaking, Socialism became an alternative and successor to Secularism. The most important national leader to make this transition was Annie Besant. In 1885 she joined the Fabians and this gave a lead to many Secularists who had been shaken by the Bradlaugh–Hyndman debate. Snell was one of the many who acknowledged the influence Mrs Besant had on him. She remained a Secularist, out of regard for Bradlaugh, until 1890, by which time her next enthusiasm, Theosophy, had completely alienated her from Foote and his followers. Between 1885 and 1890, she had continued her connection with the *National Reformer* and with the Freethought Publishing Company (which she used to publish Socialist tracts), but she was very much a freelance. She had her own papers, *Our Corner*, in which the Fabian tracts were popularised, and the *Link*. Her connection with Secularism was tenuous. In 1887 she debated 'Socialism' with Foote in the Hall of Science, City Road, and 'Individualism' with Corrie Grant in the South Place Chapel (**127**).

Mrs Besant tried to involve the Secularists in the new politics, and the National Secular Society was represented at a Fabian Conference in 1886, but Bradlaugh was out of place in the late 1880s. The ultra-radical began to look distinctly reactionary to the new generation of radical leaders. He had been a member of the International Labour Union in 1877; he spoke, at Mrs Besant's request, at the dock strike in 1889; and he was the only Liberal M.P. to speak on behalf of Cunninghame Graham in the House after the Trafalgar Square demonstration in 1887, but all this was not enough (**147**). He supported the Employer's Liability Bill of 1888, which the leading trade unionists opposed, and he opposed the Eight Hours agitation, which the unionists supported. In 1887 the S.D.F. paper, *Justice*, called Bradlaugh a Whig, and Belfort Bax later commented that Bradlaugh had become respectable on entering Parliament after 1885 (**139**). At the height of his powers, Bradlaugh had met the fate of many middle-aged reformers. He had become out of date, and as much as Secularism was built around his leadership, it too was falling behind the times.

The decline of Secularism before the growth of Socialism was a symptom also of a deeper weakness in the whole radical tradition. In the late nineteenth century eighteenth-century rationalism had lost its relevance. Those who cared to think and read deeply turned to Karl Marx, whose *Das Kapital* was translated into English in 1887. The new radicalism was concerned with social and economic problems, whereas the old had emphasised individualism and freedom of expression. The new radicalism was a political movement with representation in Parliament, while the old had belonged to an era of extra-parliamentary activity. The old radical tradition had been expressed in a number of sects rather than in a party. Owenism and Secularism had drawn on the millenarian hopes of early industrial society, and were produced by the same forces which strengthened nonconformist religion. In the late nineteenth century, both Secularism and religion were in decline. Religious aspirations were being translated into social action, and secularisation had made Secularism unnecessary.

UNIONS AND CO-OPERATION

Although the future of the Labour movement was to lie with the Socialists, this was not at all apparent from the history of the two largest components in the traditional Labour movement, the trade unions and the co-operative societies. The Secularists may have been out of touch with the new ideas, but their liberalism was shared by the co-operators and trade unionists, and they all had common roots in the ideas of Robert Owen.

Owenism as an organised movement did not survive into the second half of the nineteenth century, and the revival of co-operation after 1850 was due, in the first place, not to the infidels but to the Christian Socialists. Led by J. M. Ludlow, F. D. Maurice, Charles Kingsley, E. V. Neale and Thomas Hughes, the Christian Socialists had responded to the challenge of the 1848 revolutions by trying to assist the working classes. They pressed for legal reforms to secure the funds of co-operative societies (Slaney's Act 1852), set up a Central Co-operative Agency to supply the co-operative stores, and encouraged the establishment of co-operative working-men's associations. The latter were rarely successful, and by 1854 Christian Socialism as a formal organisation had come to an end (**52**).

Mid-Victorian England, with its general prosperity and ethos of self-help (**108**), saw a great expansion in the co-operative movement, but at the expense of co-operative principle. The profits of producer associations, such as the Co-operative Wholesale Society (founded 1863), were distributed among the customers (i.e. the co-operative

stores) and not shared with the workers themselves. This development was opposed by both the Christian Socialists and by Holyoake.
To their great surprise, Hughes, Neale and Holyoake found they
were able to make common cause in the co-partnership movement.
The old religious barriers were breaking down, and far from
appearing a threat to established society, this latterday Owenism
was seen by lords and bishops as a bulwark against the evils of state
socialism (**99, 100**).

The self-centred, apolitical attitude of self-help which characterised
the co-operative movement made it anathema to the new Socialist
leaders of the 1880s, but with 547,000 members in 1881 (1,707,000
in 1900), the co-operative movement could not be easily ignored.
Despite its outdated approach to society, it provided the means by
which the new labour movement could be spread, and the co-
operators eventually accepted the ideas of the new Socialism. In
co-operative halls and libraries throughout the country, groups of
men met and heard the familiar message of the new society expressed
in the unfamiliar language of the Fabians and the S.D.F.

The history of the trade unions was similar. The Amalgamated
Societies had set the tone of the movement since the 1850s, with their
emphasis on self-help within the capitalist system and their preference for industrial rather than political action. The more militant
unions in the coal and cotton industries were hardly the basis for
an independent labour movement. The miners were predominantly
Liberal and the cotton workers neutral or Conservative. As late as
1899 James Mawdsley of the Cotton Spinners contested Oldham as a
Conservative, and not till 1909 did all the miners throw in their lot
with the Labour Party. The leadership of the T.U.C. until the very
end of the nineteenth century was firmly in the hands of the
moderates (**138**).

The most important advocates of union militancy in the 1860s
were the Positivists—the followers of August Comte's 'Religion of
Humanity'. Led by E. S. Beesly, Frederic Harrison and Henry
Compton, they were for their decade what the Christian Socialists
had been ten years earlier. Harrison and Hughes were members of
the Royal Commission on Trade Unions (1867–69), and their
minority report was largely responsible for the improvement in the
legal status of the unions. Beesly greeted with enthusiasm the Paris
Commune in 1871, and continued to support it when even Bradlaugh
grew lukewarm. But despite these policies the Positivists were an

exotic group, and their creed was never widely accepted. They shared the same intellectual heritage as the English radicals, but they were not firmly rooted in British working-class life (**109**).

The Secularists, who were nearest to the Positivists in outlook, had very little to do with the trade union movement. The ideas of Secularism were still those of Owenism, and although Bradlaugh and Holyoake were always welcome at the Durham Miners' Gala, the Secularist leaders, with the exception of Mrs Besant, were unable to understand the changing nature of the unions, and were totally unable to grasp the significance of the development of new unionism after the late 1880s.

The economic depression of the late 1870s ended the period of prosperity and self-help. The last traces of Owenism were then lost with the failure of co-operative mining schemes, and the militancy of the Positivists and of Bradlaugh's republicanism was similarly brought to a halt.

Economic recovery in the early 1880s brought a brief revival to the old radicalism but, with a further onset of depression, the late 1880s saw the beginnings of a new radical movement, based not on one tradition—that of Paine, Carlile and Owen—but on many.

RELIGION AND THE LABOUR MOVEMENT

Looking back in his memoirs, Robert Blatchford recalled the medley of different sorts of people who made up the labour movement:

> To the I.L.P. came women and men from the ranks of Tories, Liberals, Radicals, Nonconformists and Marxians. Many of these brought with them the sectarian or party shibboleths which they had not outgrown. There were Free-Traders, Home Rulers, Local Optionists, Republicans, Roman Catholics, Salvationists, Church and Chapel-goers and believers in the cosmopolitan brotherhood of the workers (**132**).

The Secularists were agreed in their opposition to religion, but might —though usually did not—differ in their attitudes to social and political affairs. The Socialists were agreed in their attitude to social and political questions, but might—and did—differ about religion. Their leaders cover the whole spectrum of religious belief. Arthur

Henderson was a Wesleyan local preacher, active until he became Home Secretary in 1923, and a faithful chapel-goer all his life (**144**). Philip Snowden was also a Methodist, and, though he did not remain active in his membership, his life was stamped with his upbringing. He once heard Bradlaugh debate 'Has or Is Man a Soul?' with a Congregationalist minister in Burnley, but found the argument 'too abstruse for my comprehension' (**136**).

In contrast, John Burns was forced to attend Sunday school as a child, but had no religious beliefs. He joined the Secularists, but had probably never read any of the freethought classics except Paine's *Age of Reason* (**142**). H. M. Hyndman was another who viewed religion with contempt. He once described the I.L.P. as 'the queer jumble of Asiatic mysticism and supernatural juggling which we call Christianity' (**145**). Robert Blatchford was also in this tradition, and regarded orthodox Christianity as being 'a bar to intellectual progress' [**doc. 31**]. Behind these Socialists and their opposition to religion lay not only Bradlaugh and the Secularists, but also the writings of Marx and Engels. In the *Communist Manifesto* (1848) they had characterised Christian Socialism as 'the holy water with which the priest consecrates the heartburnings of the aristocrat'. Marx's concept of religion as the ideology of alienation pervades all his writings, but although he gave a theoretical justification for atheism, Marxism did not make a great impact on the British infidels.

Two other categories of Socialist leader can be described. Between the committed Christians and the out-and-out infidels are those who rejected Christianity but not religion, and those who left Christianity without rejecting it. In the former category come Harry Snell (**135**), and James Ramsay MacDonald (**146**); in the latter, Tom Mann (**134**) and Keir Hardie (**143**).

Both Snell and MacDonald were members of the Ethical Movement, which was probably the nearest religious successor to Secularism. The home of the Ethical Movement in Britain was the South Place Chapel in Finsbury. Under the ministry of W. J. Fox (1816–64) the congregation had moved from the Baptist denomination to a very liberal form of Unitarianism, and Fox's successor, Moncure D. Conway (1864–85 and 1892–97), had made the chapel the foremost home of intellectual and middle-class freethought in the country. Conway retired in 1885 to revive the reputation of Thomas Paine by writing what is still the standard *Life* (**62**, published 1892), and the chapel passed to Stanton Coit (1887–91) who completed the transformation of the congregation into an Ethical Society. In 1891 Coit left South Place to form the West London Ethical Society. Meanwhile a London Ethical Society had been founded in 1886 by Professors J. H. Muirhead and Bernard Bonsanquet under the influence of the Oxford neo-Christian philosopher, T. H. Green. In 1892 the two societies were amalgamated, and with three others, formed the Union of Ethical Societies in 1896 (**119**). Snell read Muirhead's *The Elements of Ethics* and Mazzini's *The Duty of Man*, and heard Coit and Conway at South Place in the 1890s. He even resigned his Fabian lectureship and began to lecture for the Ethical Societies in the employ of Sidney Gimson, president of the Leicester Secular Society, who was trying to spread the Ethical Movement in the provinces. MacDonald also lectured to the Ethical Societies, and, in 1898 with Coit and J. A. Hobson, he formed the Society of Ethical Propagandists. Whereas Burns, with his contempt for both religion and intellectual freethought, represents one side of the radical infidel tradition, MacDonald and Snell represent the other. When Snell later wrote that he was attracted to the Ethical Movement by 'its proposal to establish in the world a religion of devotion to the ideal of a righteousness without supernatural sanctions' (**135**) he was using words which Holyoake and many Secularists, Owen and many Owenites, Paine and the Theophilanthropists, would have found impeccable.

The Ethical Movement was strongest in London, whilst in the provinces Nonconformity made what was probably the strongest single impact on the labour movement. Tom Mann was a Birmingham engineer, who went to Bible classes run by a Quaker, attended Temperance meetings on Saturday evenings, and went to church twice on Sundays where he was a Sunday school teacher. He was influenced by Holyoake, but his dislike of the Churches arose from their opposition to social reform. Where he found helpful clergymen, he responded to them and helped them in return. He lectured in Nonconformist chapels, and at one time it was rumoured that he was about to take orders and become curate to the Reverend Thorry Gardiner at St George's-in-the-Borough (**134**). Keir Hardie was another Socialist with strong Christian sympathies. His parents became freethinkers when he was a small boy in Glasgow, and the works of Ingersoll, the American freethinker, and Paine's *Age of Reason* were in the house, but through the Temperance movement, Keir joined the Good Templars and the Evangelical Union, and his later work with the I.L.P. reflected these influences (**143**) [**doc. 32**].

Whatever their religious differences, the Socialists brought to their new movement some of their former sectarian beliefs. Socialism, like Owenism and Secularism, had many of the characteristics of a new religion (for non-Christians) or of a purified religion (for Christians). Like the Secularist and Co-operative movements, the Socialists had their Sunday schools. They even had their conversions: Philip Snowden used to appeal to men and women to come to the front and sign as members of the I.L.P. This was popularly known as 'Philip's come to Jesus' (**148**).

The most obviously religious form which the Socialist movement took was that of the Labour Churches, described by William Walsh in 1891 as 'the New Secularism' (**42**). The first Labour Church was founded in Manchester in 1891 by John Trevor, a Unitarian minister who was dissatisfied with theology but believed in God and was appalled by the gulf which existed between the orthodox Churches and the working classes. His Church had religious ceremonies, but the 'sermons' were really political speeches. Its importance was that it provided a stepping-stone for some Nonconformists on their way to Socialism. There were never more than thirty places of worship, but, unlike the Ethical Societies with which the Labour Churches were associated in the Ethical Union, they were well scattered throughout the provinces. The Labour Churches, however, failed to live up to Trevor's expectations, and they gradually lost their religious characteristics. By 1914 they were virtually extinct (**138**). Like the orthodox sects, the labour sects appealed to religious sentiments which were losing their significance both in radical politics and in everyday life (**140, 25**).

RELIGION AND THE WORKING CLASSES IN 1900

The second half of the nineteenth century had appeared to be a time of great expansion for the Churches. In 1900 there were more buildings and more people in the pews than fifty years earlier, and yet the health of the Church was a statistical illusion. Between 1851 and 1881 the proportion of estimated church attenders to the total population remained constant at about one in four. The Church was barely keeping pace with the increase in population and the growth in numbers merely reflected the doubling of the population between

1851 and 1901. Buildings appeared to be fuller because the number of sittings available had increased by only 40 per cent in the same period. The rate of growth had, in fact, levelled off, and towards the end of the century signs of decline became apparent. Different areas of the country and different denominations were affected in different ways. In Sheffield, for example, where the population more than doubled between 1851 and 1881, the number of Anglican worshippers increased by 130 per cent, but the Wesleyan Methodists by only 10 per cent. The total numbers in all Methodist groups (excluding the Salvation Army), however, did double, and the Baptists and Congregationalists were really the denominations to fall behind (**48**). This weakness of Dissent in Sheffield, though, was probably not typical of the country as a whole. In London between 1886 and 1902 (when censuses of religious worship were conducted by the *British Weekly* and the *Daily News* respectively) the Anglican Church declined severely (**40**). In the metropolis, the total estimated number of attendances at all churches fell by about 150,000 despite an increase in population of over 500,000, and nearly all this decline can be accounted for by the weakness of the Church of England. The Methodists staved off a similar decline only by abandoning their circuit system and basing their work on central mission halls. 'The Forward Movement has saved London Methodism', wrote Jane T. Stoddart in a comparison of the two censuses. 'A new world has been called into existence to redress the balance of the old' (**40**).

The new world, however, was not to be one populated with Methodist missions and Baptist tabernacles. More significant than the decline in old institutions was the decay in attitudes. Even where revival did occur, as in South Wales in 1904, the event can be interpreted as a reaction against the progressive secularisation of life (**56**). The old radical alliance of chapel, co-operative store and people was passing away. When Beatrice Webb stayed with her working-class relatives in Bacup (east Lancashire) in the early 1880s, she perceived this tendency and wondered what would take the place of the old puritan idealism (**137, 53**).

The answer was concern with economic improvement, and new class demands which cut across the old communities, such as Mrs Webb had noted in Bacup or which endured in the valleys of South Wales (**46**). The Nonconformist capitalist could no longer represent the interests of his Nonconformist workpeople. If he did not move to the parish church and the Tory Party, they left the chapel altogether and joined the Labour Party. The Bradford Labour Church and the Bradford Labour Union were symbols of the breakdown of the old radical alliance based on Liberalism and the chapel.

Paradoxically, this decline of the Church in statistical terms and in the eyes of the Labour movement, was accompanied by a growing sympathy within the Churches for the Labour movement. In 1851 the Christian Socialists were a tiny and eccentric minority within the Establishment, but by the end of the century, large numbers of clergymen regarded themselves as being Christian Socialists in some sense or other. The Settlement Movement had brought the middle classes and the universities into contact with the grim realities of working-class life in the slums; older sources of antagonism, like clerical magistrates and church rates, were things of the past. The principles of the early Christian Socialists had become almost commonplaces [**doc. 33**], and the social involvement of the Church of England was affirmed by successive Lambeth Conferences after 1888. The Roman Catholics, under Manning's influence, were also closely involved in social and labour questions, and William Booth's Salvation Army began to see the spiritual problems of London in social terms. Booth's startling book, *In Darkest London and the Way Out* (1890), was concerned as much with physical as with spiritual destitution, and prescribed as a remedy a plan for home colonies of which Owenites could have approved.

In a way, this was typical of the reaction of the Churches to the problems of labour. Religious philanthropists, and, indeed, Liberal politicians, were trying to apply outdated remedies to a changed situation, and the religious press became increasingly hostile to the new Socialism when in the years immediately before the First World War Christians realised its revolutionary implications. Dissent, in its traditional place on the left wing of the Liberal Party, was growing increasingly irrelevant. The 1906 general election was one of the last occasions when it exercised any real power, over the scandal of Chinese indentured labour in South Africa. The 1902 Education Act was the last such measure to be widely denounced on the old anti-State Church grounds (**53**). The voice of Lloyd George continued to ring round the hills of Wales, but the radicalism for which he stood was dead (**23**).

The modern, secular Labour movement owes much to the old radical tradition, but it was no mere continuation of that tradition.

The old looked back to the Enlightenment and the French Revolution; its hero was Thomas Paine. It sometimes looked back even further, to the Commonwealth and the radical republicanism of the Puritan sects; the name of Cromwell was frequently on the lips of nineteenth-century orators. The militant freethinkers of the school of Paine, and the dissenting chapels and sects, were alike parts of this tradition. But religion was losing its hold on the culture of the people in the late nineteenth century. The Church had failed to win the working classes; now it was losing the middle classes as well. The decay of organised religion, the decline of the Liberal Party, the weakening of the Nonconformist conscience, the virtual disappearance of militant Secularism, and, later and indirectly, the decline of the co-operative movement, can all be seen as aspects of that comprehensive change which became noticeable at the end of the nineteenth century—the disappearance of the old style of radical politics in which religion and unbelief played so great a part, and the end of the radical tradition.

Part Four

DOCUMENTS

I. RELIGION AND THE WORKING CLASSES

document 1

The Religious Census, 1851

The first half of the nineteenth century was a time of general religious expansion, but the churches were painfully aware that they were not attracting many of the working classes. The Religious Census, taken on 30 March 1851, confirmed this failure.

The most important fact which this investigation as to attendance brings before us is, unquestionably, the alarming number of non-attendants. Even in the least unfavorable aspect of the figures just presented, and assuming (as no doubt is right) that the 5,288,294 absent every Sunday are not always the same individuals, it must be apparent that a sadly formidable portion of the English people are habitual neglecters of the public ordinances of religion. Nor is it difficult to indicate to what particular class of the community this portion in the main belongs. The middle classes have augmented rather than diminished that devotional sentiment and strictness of attention to religious services by which, for several centuries, they have so eminently been distinguished. With the upper classes, too, the subject of religion has obtained of late a marked degree of notice, and a regular church-attendance is now ranked among the recognized proprieties of life. It is to satisfy the wants of these two classes that the number of religious structures has of late years so increased. But while the *labouring* myriads of our country have been multiplying with our multiplied material prosperity, it cannot, it is feared, be stated that a corresponding increase has occurred in the attendance of this class in our religious edifices. More especially in cities and large towns it is observable how absolutely insignificant a portion of the congregations is composed of artizans. They fill, perhaps, in youth, our National, British, and Sunday Schools, and there receive the elements of a religious education; but, no sooner do they mingle in the active world of labour than, subjected to the constant action of opposing influences, they soon become as utter strangers to religious ordinances as the people of a heathen country. From whatever cause, in them or in the manner of their treatment by religious bodies, it is sadly certain that this vast, intelligent, and growingly important section of our countrymen is thoroughly estranged from our religious institutions in their present aspect. Probably, indeed, the prevalence of *infidelity* has been exaggerated, if the word be taken in its popular meaning, as implying some degree of intellectual effort and decision; but, no doubt, a great extent of negative, inert indifference prevails, the practical effects of which are much the same. There is a sect, originated recently, adherents to a system called "Secularism"; the principal tenet being that, as the fact of a future life is (in their view) at all events susceptible of *some* degree of doubt, while the fact and the necessities of a present life are matters of direct sensation, it is therefore prudent to attend exclusively to the concerns of that existence which is certain and immediate—not wasting energies required for present duties by a preparation for remote, and merely possible, contingencies. This is the creed which probably with most exactness indicates the faith which, virtually though not professedly, is entertained by the masses of our working population; by the skilled and unskilled labourer alike—by hosts of minor shopkeepers and Sunday traders—and by miserable denizens of courts and crowded alleys. They are *unconscious Secularists*—engrossed by the demands, the trials, or the pleasures of the passing hour, and ignorant or careless of a future. These are never or but seldom seen in our religious congregations; and the melancholy fact is thus impressed upon our notice that the classes which are most in need of the restraints and consolations of religion are the classes which are most without them.

From Horace Mann (**39**).

document 2

Religion and reform

The Churches and the Bible were condemned by radical lecturers as obstacles to reform. The following is taken from the end of a course of lectures given by Robert Cooper, the Manchester Owenite and Secularist.

Possibly in these discourses I may have employed, when speaking of the clerical profession, strong expressions of reproach and denunciation. Let it be understood that on all such occasions I spoke of them as an *organisation* rather than as individuals, as a *system* rather than as *men*. There are honourable exceptions I am proud to admit; but as a *class*, willingly or unwillingly on their part, they are the stumbling-block in the way of every effort to enlighten and emancipate mankind. Talk of *social* reform, and they exclaim that poverty is a *divine* ordinance; that God made both *poor* and rich, and the people must, therefore, 'be content in the situation in which Divine Providence has placed them'. Talk of *political* reform, and they remind you that it is our duty, by command of the inspired word of heaven, to submit 'to the powers that be'. Talk of *educational* progress, and they exclaim that all education without religion, which simply means without *them*, 'would be a curse rather than a blessing'. Talk of *moral* reform in the shape of the temperance or any other kindred movement, and they caution us to quote the words of the Rev. Mr Duncan, of North Shields, that 'it is an attempt to take the regeneration of man out of God's hands'. Talk of *peace* reform, and we behold the mitred priest blessing the fatal emblem of human slaughter. Talk of reform in the blackest, the vilest, the meanest of all mortal abuses, the selling of human flesh, the trading in human slavery, and the man of God points his finger to the infallible page sanctioning the crime! Oh if the humble efforts I have made in these lectures have only contributed to check, however feebly, this monstrous power—to snap one link in the chain of human oppression, to shed one beam of light upon human ignorance, to force one step in advance the glorious car of progress, I can at least leave the world 'better for having lived in it'.

From Robert Cooper, *The Immortality of the Soul*, London, 1853, p. 100.

document 3

Superstition in the countryside

Popular religion in the countryside, even when called 'Christianity', often amounted to no more than pagan superstition based on the credulity of the people. The following is a description of Herne Hill, Broughton and Dunkirk, in Kent, where 'Mad Thoms' led a peasants' rising in 1838, and was supported by a number of people who believed him to be Christ.

The kind of education received by these persons was of the lowest and most inefficient description. . . . Very few could write their own names; and those who could read, rarely ventured upon any other book than the Testament or Bible. Indeed, the usual answer in the district to the question "Can you read?" is, "Yes, a little in the Testament."

The houses generally appear to be tolerably provided with Bibles and Testaments, but beyond these and a few tracts scarcely a book is to be found in a cottage in the district. That these are not mere random assertions, hazarded from a hasty glance at a few cottages, will appear from the details given further on, and which are the result of a careful and minute investigation. A little consideration of the nature of rural life will show the danger of leaving the peasantry in such a state of ignorance. In the solitude of the country, the uncultivated mind is much more open to the impressions of fanaticism than in the bustle and collision of towns. In such a stagnant state of existence the mind acquires no activity, and is unaccustomed to make those investigations and comparisons necessary to detect imposture. The slightest semblance of evidence is often sufficient with them to support a deceit which elsewhere would not have the smallest chance of escaping detection. If we look for a moment at the absurdities and inconsistencies practised by Thoms, it appears at first utterly inconceivable that any persons out of a lunatic asylum could have been deceived by him. At one time he had assumed the title of Baron Rothschild, at another of the Earl of Devon, then of King of Jerusalem, and afterwards of a knight of Malta;—and all these absurdities had been openly practised before the eyes of the very persons among whom he afterwards ventured to appear as the Saviour of the world. To support this last assumption, his chief advantages were a commanding person and a handsome countenance, which he made in some degree to resemble the common portraits of Christ, by wearing his hair parted at the crown, and a long flowing beard. To these advantages were joined a considerable fluency of speech, and the power of interlarding his discourse with Scriptural phraseology. That an imposture so gross and so slenderly supported should have succeeded, must teach us, if anything will, the folly and danger of leaving the agricultural population in the debasing ignorance which now exists among them.

From F. Liardet, 'State of the peasantry in the county of Kent' in *Report of the Central Society for Education*, iii, London, 1839, 87–139.

Unbelief in the towns

document 4

Among the most reliable descriptions of the urban working classes are the reports of the Unitarian Domestic Missionaries. They confirm the picture given by Horace Mann in **doc. 1.**

A few remarks on the relation between Christian churches and the labouring population may not unsuitably be here introduced. The bulk of the people in humble circumstances, do not attend any place of worship, or observe any religious forms, with the exception of those connected with baptisms, marriages and funerals. They appear, for the most part, to have lost all interest in the public celebration of divine worship. Most of those who do still value Christian privileges belong, I think, to the churches of England and Rome, and these probably will be found on inquiry to be the denominations which take most pains, in this town, at least, to attract and attach them. Let me not, however, be supposed to say that the great mass of the working classes have no religion. Many of them have a religious feeling, of a rude and peculiar character, dormant and uninfluential, indeed, in ordinary circumstances, and little addicted to public, or perhaps, to any acts of habitual devotion, but which, nevertheless restrains them from much evil, and awakens their hopes and fears in times of affliction. This is the case with the majority; but modern enlightenment has produced another party, who, confounding piety with its abuses, and vain of their own superiority to superstition, treat all religion as a "cunningly devised fable". It is extremely difficult to make any satisfactory impression on either of these classes. The one is armed in ignorance, the other in conceit, so as to be almost impervious to ordinary influences.

From the Manchester Ministry to the Poor, *Annual Report*, 1848, pp. 25–6.

It must not be supposed from what I have said, that there are none, or very few, among the working classes, who attend from conviction and choice to their religious duties. There are some of these, I trust, in connexion with every Christian congregation in the town. My object has been simply to shew how the labouring population stand affected towards religion, and particularly towards Christianity. The substance of my testimony on this head is to the following effect. The *great majority* of the working people here are not in the habit of attending any place of worship. But this majority is made up of *three* unequal sections. One considerable division consists of such as, in the main, are upright, well-meaning Christians, who either from a want of sympathy with existing modes of conducting religious services, from hindrances in their own circumstances, over which they have little control, or, perhaps, very often from culpable neglect, do not usually frequent the house of prayer. A much larger class consists of ignorant, worldly-minded, sensual people, who, without having taken the trouble to reject Christianity, are habitually regardless of its claims. The remaining section, which is smaller, but more energetic than either of these, account all religion a delusion, and consider it very much in the light of an enemy to their liberties and their pleasures. Thus, the *non-professing, the indifferent*, and *the unbelieving classes*, in something like the proportions I have indicated, make up the great majority of the labouring population who are not in the habit of attending any of our places of worship. There still remains *the minority*, which outnumbers probably any one of the above classes but the indifferent, and comprises Christians of all denominations. Many of these are persons of great excellence; who bear their trials with exemplary fortitude, and, in our

Sunday schools, as well as in their daily walks of duty, labour with self-devotion and earnestness to do good.

From the Manchester Ministry to the Poor, *Annual Report*, 1850, pp. 55–6.

document 5
The working classes

Among the lower orders of society there was a clear division between the artisan élite of the working classes, and the labouring poor. Religious and radical organisations alike were rarely the concern of this latter group.

What were the amusements of the masses, thus over-worked, ill-fed, ill-housed,—left for the most part uneducated? Large numbers of working people attended fairs and wakes, at the latter of which jumping in sacks, climbing greased poles, grinning through horse-collars for tobacco, hunting pigs with soaped tails, were the choicest diversions. An almost general unchastity—the proofs of which are as abundant as they would be painful to adduce—prevailed amongst the women employed in factories, and generally throughout the lowest ranks of the working population. But drink was the mainspring of enjoyment. When Saturday evening came, indulgences began which continued till Sunday evening. Fiddles were to be heard on all sides, and limp-looking men and pale-faced women thronged the public-houses, and reeled and jigged till they were turned, drunk and riotous, into the streets, at most unseasonable hours. On the Sunday morning the public-houses were again thronged, that the thirst following the indulgence of the night might be quenched. When church hour approached, however, the churchwardens, with long staves tipped with silver, sallied forth, and, when possible, seized all the drunken and unkempt upon whom they could lay their hands, and these, being carefully lodged in a pew provided for them, were left there to enjoy the sermon, whilst their captors usually adjourned to some tavern near at hand, for the purpose of rewarding themselves with a glass or two for the important services they had rendered to morality and religion. In fact, sullen, silent work alternated with noisy, drunken riot; and Easter and Whitsuntide debauches, with an occasional outbreak during some favourite "wakes", rounded the whole life of the factory worker.

The ordinary artisan of the workshop was, indeed, a far different man. He was not tied down to the routine of a huge mechanical system, so expensive, whether at rest or in motion, that to be profitable it needed the regular aid of human labour. His freedom of intercouse with his fellow-workman was almost unrestricted. He had time for study, when inclined; and if he preferred the public-house to the workshop—which he too often did—it was a matter of choice, and he was open to correction when any sufficient influence could be brought to bear upon him. Besides, he was not put to work at so early an age, and, as a rule, had received more education, and experienced more fully the benefit of home influence. . . . There were grave men, who employed their leisure hours in reading or study—entomologists, florists, botanists, students in chemistry and astronomy. Men were there—politicians, dabblers in theology—. . . Individual character was very strongly marked amongst these men. Some of them in their trades' meetings, when speaking on subjects familiar to them by experience, were eloquent, logical, and powerful orators; some quiet and business-like and clever in negotiation; others, again, were as ingeniously unprincipled as if they had been born to rule empires, full of quips and quillets.

From Lloyd Jones, the Manchester Owenite, in J. M. Ludlow and Lloyd Jones, *Progress of the Working Class, 1832–1867*, London, 1867. For a similar portrait of Manchester life in fiction, see Mrs Gaskell (**150**).

II. THE ORIGINS OF THE RADICAL TRADITION

Deism and Christianity contrasted

Thomas Paine presented in vivid and popular language the arguments of the eighteenth-century reformers in political and religious affairs. His witty irreverence endeared him to the members of the radical clubs in the 1790s, and his works were reprinted and widely read and quoted throughout the nineteenth century.

Of all the systems of religion that ever were invented, there is none more derogatory to the Almighty, more unedifying to man, more repugnant to reason, and more contradictory in itself, than this thing called Christianity. Too absurd for belief, too impossible to convince, and too inconsistent for practice, it renders the heart torpid, or produces only atheists and fanatics. As an engine of power, it serves the purpose of despotism; and as a means of wealth, the avarice of priests; but so far as respects the good of man in general, it leads to nothing here, or hereafter.

The only religion that has not been invented, and that has in it every evidence of divine originality, is pure and simple deism. It must have been the first, and will probably be the last that man believes. But pure and simple deism does not answer the purpose of despotic governments. They cannot lay hold of religion as an engine, but by mixing it with human inventions, and making their own authority a part; neither does it answer the avarice of priests, but by incorporating themselves and their functions with it, and becoming, like the government, a party in the system. It is this that forms the otherwise mysterious connection of church and state; the church humane, and the state tyrannic.

Were a man impressed as fully and as strongly as he ought to be, with the belief of a God, his moral life would be regulated by the force of this belief: he would stand in awe of God, and of himself, and would not do the thing that could not be concealed from either. To give this belief the full opportunity of force, it is necessary that it acts alone. This is deism.

But when, according to the Christian Trinitarian scheme, one part of God is represented by a dying man, and another part, called the Holy Ghost, by a flying pigeon, it is impossible that belief can attach itself to such wild conceits.

It has been the scheme of the Christian church, and of all the other invented systems of religion, to hold man in ignorance of the Creator, as it is of government to hold him in ignorance of his rights. The systems of the one are as false as those of the other, and are calculated for mutual support. The study of theology, as it stands in Christian churches, is the study of nothing; it is founded on nothing; it rests on no principles; it proceeds by no authorities; it has no data; it can demonstrate nothing; and admits of no conclusion. Not any thing can be studied as a science, without our being in possession of the principles upon which it is founded; and as this is not the case with Christian theology, it is therefore the study of nothing.

Instead then of studying theology, as is now done, out of the Bible and Testament, the meanings of which books are always controverted, and the authenticity of which is disproved, it is necessary that we refer to the Bible of the creation. The principles we discover there, are eternal, and of divine origin: they are the foundation of all the science that exists in the world, and must be the foundation of theology.

We can know God only through his works. We cannot have a conception of any one attribute, but by following some principle that leads to it. We have only a confused idea of his power, if we have not the means of comprehending something of it's [sic] immensity. We can have no idea of his wisdom, but by knowing the order and manner in which it acts. The principles of science lead to this knowledge; for the Creator of man is the Creator of science, and it is through that medium that man can see God, as it were, face to face.

From Thomas Paine, *The Age of Reason, Part the Second, being an Investigation of True and Fabulous Theology*, 2nd edn, London, 1795, pp. 102–3.

The political clubs

The political clubs of the 1790s spread the radical ideas contained in the writings of Thomas Paine and others. The government in Britain therefore regarded them with great suspicion.

In the whole course of their inquiry, your Committee have found the clearest proofs of a systematic design, long since adopted and acted upon by France, in conjunction with domestic traitors, and pursued up to the present moment with unabated perseverance, to overturn the laws, constitution, and government, and every existing establishment, civil or ecclesiastical, both in Great Britain and Ireland; as well as to dissolve the connexion between the two kingdoms, so necessary to the security and prosperity of both.

The chief hope of accomplishing this design, has rested on the propagation of those destructive principles, which originally produced the French Revolution, with all the miseries and calamities since experienced in France, and now extended over a large part of Europe.

The most effectual engine employed for this purpose, has been the institution of political societies, of a nature and description before unknown in any country, and inconsistent with public tranquillity, and with the existence of regular government. . . .

It can hardly be necessary to recall to the recollection of the House, the industry with which they endeavoured to disseminate these sentiments by the circulation of their own proceedings and resolutions; uniformly directed to vilify the forms and principles of the British constitution; to represent the people of this country as groaning under intolerable oppression; to eradicate all religious principle; and to recommend a recurrence to experiments of desperate innovation similar to those which were at that time adopted in France. For the same purpose, the works of Paine, and other seditious and impious publications, were distributed, throughout almost every part of the kingdom, with an activity and profusion beyond all former example.

So confident were the societies of the efficacy of these measures, that they appear almost universally to have looked forward from the beginning, to the entire overthrow of every existing establishment in these kingdoms, and to the creation of some democratical form of government; either by uniting the whole of the British empire into one republic, or by dividing it into two or more republics.

From *Report from the Committee of Secrecy of the House of Commons relative to the Proceedings of different Persons and Societies in Great Britain and Ireland engaged in a Treasonable Conspiracy*, 15 March [1799], *Hansard*, lxxxiv, cols. 579–80, 584.

document 8

Anticlericalism and republicanism

A colourful, though heavily biased, picture of some of these political societies is given in a pamphlet by W. H. Reid, who claimed to be writing from personal experience.

Vain glory, and a blind resentment, as silly as it is savage, often hurry men into the wildest extremes.—I am an Atheist! exclaimed one of those persons, and, jumping upon a club-room table; here, said he, holding up an infant, here is a young Atheist! Another, to shew how little he regarded the Bible, observed, at another meeting, "That just before he came from home, he kicked something before him, and, picking it up, what should it be but an old Bible; that, till then, he did not know he had any such thing in his house!" A third philosopher, censuring the present mode of education, observed, "There would never be any good done, till towns and cities were built without a single church, chapel, or any place of worship, in them!" Another member, being weary of the deliberations at which he was present, exclaimed, *"What signifies our sitting here? let us go and kill all the bl—dy priests!"*

From W. H. Reid (**57**).

III. THE BLASPHEMOUS AND SEDITIOUS PRESS

document 9

The Blasphemous and Seditious Libels Act, 1819

Of all the reactionary legislation passed by Parliament during and after the revolutionary wars, the Act which most symbolised repression was that one of the Six Acts of 1819 which extended the Stamp Laws to include the popular cheap press. The radicals never ceased to demand its repeal, but the Association for the Repeal of the Taxes on Knowledge did not achieve this aim until 1869–70.

An Act to subject certain Publications to the Duties of Stamps upon Newspapers, and to make other Regulations for restraining the Abuses arising from the Publication of blasphemous and seditious Libels.

Whereas Pamphlets and printed Papers containing Observations upon public Events and Occurrences, tending to excite Hatred and Contempt of the Government and Constitution of these Realms as by Law established, and also vilifying our Holy Religion, have lately been published in great Numbers, and at very small Prices; and it is expedient that the same should be restrained: May it therefore please Your Majesty that it may be enacted; and be it enacted by the King's most Excellent Majesty, . . . That from and after Ten Days after the passing of this Act, all Pamphlets and Papers containing any Public News, Intelligence or Occurrences, or any Remarks or Observations thereon, or upon any Matter in Church or State, printed in any Part of the United Kingdom for Sale, and published periodically, or in Parts or Numbers, at Intervals not exceeding Twenty-six Days between the Publication of any Two such Pamphlets or Papers, Parts or Numbers, where any of the said Pamphlets or Papers, Parts or Numbers respectively, shall not exceed Two Sheets, or shall be published for Sale for a less Sum than Sixpence, exclusive of the Duty by this Act imposed thereon, shall be deemed and taken to be Newspapers within the true Intent and Meaning of an Act of Parliament passed in the Thirty-eighth Year of the Reign of His present Majesty, . . . and all other Acts of Parliament in force relating to Newspapers; . . .

IV. And be it further enacted, That all Pamphlets and Papers containing any Public News, Intelligence, or Occurrences, or any such Remarks or Observations as aforesaid, ... shall be first published on the First Day of every Calendar Month, or within Two Days before or after that Day, and at no other Time; and that if any Person or Persons shall first publish or cause to be published any such Pamphlet, Paper, Part or Number aforesaid, on any other Day or Time, he or they shall forfeit for every such Offence the Sum of Twenty Pounds.

From the Act of 60 George III, cap. 9 [30 December 1819].

document 10

The Fleet Street struggle (1822)

Carlile's shop in Fleet Street was kept open during his imprisonment in the early 1820s by scores of volunteers. They used every stratagem to avoid conviction, but when caught, they demonstrated their contempt for the law and used their trials to win further support for their cause.

I will give as correct an account as memory will enable me to do. . . . I shall commence at the time when Miss Mary Ann Carlile was imprisoned. Calling, as I usually did, on a Saturday evening, I found her in great trouble, when I inquired 'what was the cause of her trouble?' Her answer was, that 'next week she was to surrender, to receive sentence of the Court, and be imprisoned. Then the House in Fleet Street would be closed, and they would be starved in prison.' It struck me forcibly that this would most probably be their fate, knowing the apathy that generally follows after a person gets into prison. It completely staggered me for the moment, that I hardly knew how to answer, for I saw that what she anticipated would inevitably be the case. After considering for a minute or two, I asked her if she knew any one that she thought would meet me, at 55, Fleet Street, on the next Monday evening? Her answer was, she thought she knew one. I told her to get him to come, and I would be sure to be there at eight o'clock precisely.

At this time I used to have on a Sunday afternoon a few Atheistical friends to meet at my house, and have tea; and after tea we used to read and discuss—in this way we used to amuse ourselves for the evening.

When my friends arrived on the Sunday evening, after I had seen Miss M. A. Carlile, and our tea was over, I informed them in what predicament Mr. Carlile and family stood; and that I thought we ought not to let that be the case; that we should endeavour to keep the House open at all hazards, and do our best towards finding funds for the maintenance of Mr. Carlile and family . . .

Mrs. Susannah Wright volunteered to take charge of the House, and attend to the business at all risk, and we, on our part, agreed to support her; . . .

Mr. Carlile had formed a plan to sell the books down a spout, so that the person purchasing the books could not see the person that sold them. In this way it was accomplished:—There was a little door on the counter, which the person wanting a book had to rap at, when the door opened, and the purchaser asked for the book which he wanted. Then a small bag was lowered down for the money. When it was drawn up, the book with the change—if any was required—was lowered down to the purchaser. By this system the informers were baffled; and Mr. C. was enabled to carry on his business, and also to collect subscriptions from the different parts of the country direct, without passing through the hands of the committee, which was of essential service to him, in case of his shop being closed. In this way his business was carried on for some time; and the Government, with the 'Bridge Street Gang', as they were called, were thus foiled, till at length the Government made a seizure; and by that means closed the House, 55, Fleet Street. But this was but of short duration, for we found another house not far from the other, which I took in my name. I saw the landlord, and agreed to take the house. I gave him reference to the landlord that I was then living under, which was so far satisfactory that he accepted me as his tenant. When I had got possession, I let the first floor to Mr. Carlile, when Mrs. S. Wright took her abode there, and Mr. Carlile's business was carried on as usual.

From B. B. Jones, 'The people's first struggle for free speech and writing. Led by Richard Carlile. In which they were completely successful', *Reasoner*, xxiv, no. 680, 5 June 1859, pp. 178–9.

Religion and science

Belief in Reason and Natural Law was fundamental to the philosophers of the Enlightenment, and Richard Carlile adopted this rationalistic creed in preference to that offered by the priests. He expressed it in a style which was both provocative and popular.

What avail the dogmas of the priest about an end to the world, about a resurrection, about a day of judgement, about a Heaven and Hell, or about rewards and punishments after this life, when we assert that matter is imperishable and indestructible—that it always was what it now is, and that it will always continue the same. Answer this, ye Priests. Come forward, ye Men of Science, and support these plain truths, which are as familiar to your minds, as the simplest demonstration in mathematics is to the experienced and accomplished mathematician. Future rewards and punishments are cried up as a neccessary doctrine wherewith to impress the minds of men, and to restrain them from vice: but how much more impressive and comprehensible would be the plain and simple truth, that, in this life, virtue produces happiness, and vice nothing but certain misery.

All religious notions in all their degrees must properly be termed a species of madness. Whatever opinions prevail in the minds of men which have no foundation in Nature, or natural laws, they can merit no other designation than insanity. Insanity, or madness, consists in unnatural or incoherent thoughts and actions, therefore, as no species of religious notions have any alliance with nature, it is but a just inference to say, that they individually or collectively comprise the term *madness*. ... Reason, or a knowledge of nature, is the only specific for it, and he who can throw the greatest quantity into the social system will prove the best physician. Several quacks have made pretensions to give society relief from this madness but they have only tortured the patient without checking the disease. Thomas Paine, and a few American and French physicians, have been the only ones to treat it in an effectual manner, and by the use of their recipes, and the assistance of MEN OF SCIENCE, I hope at least effectually to destroy the contagious part of the disease.

From Richard Carlile, *An Address to Men of Science; calling upon them to stand forward and Vindicate the Truth from the Foul Grasp and Persecution of Superstition; and obtain for the Island of Great Britain the noble appellation of the Focus of Truth; whence mankind shall be illuminated, and the black and pestiferous clouds of Persecution and Superstition be banished from the face of the earth; as the only sure prelude to Universal Peace and Harmony among the Human Race. In which a Sketch of a Proper System for the Education of Youth is submitted to their judgement*, London, 1821, pp. 7, 25–6.

document 12

Blasphemy at the Rotunda

Robert Taylor, the 'Devil's Chaplain', mocked Christianity in the style of the most popular ultra-radical agitators, but at the same time he was able to bring to his 'sermons' a wealth of learning. The following extracts are from works prosecuted for blasphemy.

In the full tide of evangelical declamation, the fathers of our English church, pursuing to its full extent the dogma of the absolute divinity of Christ, in commemoration of this day, which they call *Good Friday*, to this effect, address their admiring congregations:—

"Carry back your minds, ye faithful Christians, to the aweful scenes of Gethsemane and Calvary. He who suffered on that bitter cross, was none other than the Creator of the world himself. O aweful mystery! O love divine! there you behold the Almighty God arraigned as a felon at the bar of Pontius Pilate. Him, who only hath immortality, tried for his life; Jesus Christ, *the righteous*, found guilty: the author of nature, suffered: the Immortal God, expired: the Everlasting, ceased to be: the Eternal, was no more: the Great *I am*, was *not*: the living God, was dead. There was a radical reform in the Kingdom of Heaven; the boroughmongers were turned out; the Jure-Divino-ship of God himself was no longer respected; '*God over all,*' was put under; '*Blessed for evermore,*' was no more blessed; 'Holy, Holy, Holy,' was wholly kicked out; 'Jehovah's aweful

107

throne,' was declared vacant; and the provisional government devolved into the hands of that venerable old republican, Lieutenant-General Beelzebub."

From a sermon delivered by Robert Taylor on Good Friday, 1830, and printed in the *Devil's Pulpit*, no. 14, 3 June 1831, p. 210.

All our churches and chapels to this day are built, as all the Pagan Pagodas and Temples of the Sun, through unrecorded ages, were, so as to have their altars in the East: and all the light allowed to fall on that mystic table, was such alone as could gleam through that window in the East, darkened[,] obscured, and shaded, as much as conveniently might be, by the cultivated growth of IVY, trained to grow on the church wall, and to spread its dark foliage, as a leafy umbrella, over that sacred window; the *Ivy*, before the invention of glass, serving to keep off the showers, or to prevent too much light from shining on the mysteries of that dark table, there being nothing that the priests, whether Pagan or Christian, Catholic or Protestant, were ever so much afraid of, as of letting in too much light upon their Sacraments.

But the *Ivy*, sirs! Why is *Ivy* trained, to this day, to grow in Christian church-yards, and to spread its leaves over the eastern window, immediately over the sacred table, and sacred *"Cup of Salvation,"* standing on that sacred table in, "the order for the administration of the Holy Communion," but because *Ivy* was the peculiar emblem of the Jolly God, Bacchus, who is always represented as crowned with a garland of Ivy-leaves? And Bacchus and Christ Jesus were never more different from each other, than six and a half-dozen,—or, than different versions of the same substantive allegory—JE*sus* [*sic*] being indisputably one of the names of Bacchus.

From a sermon delivered by Robert Taylor on Easter Sunday, 1830, at which Taylor enacted the Easter Communion; printed in the *Devil's Pulpit*, no. 15, 10 June 1831, pp. 227–8.

Priestianity and Christianity

A common approach to religion made by the radical lecturers was to attack the institutional forms of Christianity in the name of 'real' Christianity.

When hypocrisy and coercion is made to give way to sincerity, truth, freedom, and fraternal affection, men will understand the religion of Jesus. They will have seen their *present*, and will be secure of their *future* and *eternal* salvation; but this glorious consummation will not arrive till *priestcraft* receives its death-blow from the intelligence, good sense, and virtue of the people at large. What is now the great obstacle to the mental, moral, social, and political improvement of the people?—PRIESTCRAFT, or PRIESTIANITY. The priests of all religions, and of all sects, thrive by deluding the people. They live by teaching *false doctrines*, and by proscribing all false doctrines but their own, and those who believe in them. This practice promotes division and separation among the people, instead of uniting them in the bonds of "brotherly affection". This is not the religion of Jesus. It is not *Christianity*; it is *Priestianity*, which has caused more disputations and ill-will than, perhaps, any subject that ever arrested the attention of a human being. I say *Priestianity*, because genuine *Christianity*, the religion taught by Jesus, is, as I have clearly shown, a plain, practical religion, unpolluted with mysteries, unencumbered with priests, and eminently calculated to generate in the minds of its sincere votaries, a love of truth, of justice, and of liberty.

From Henry Hetherington, *Cheap Salvation; or, an Antidote to Priestcraft*, London, [1832?], p. 17.

IV. OWENISM

Owen on religion

Robert Owen began to publicise his views in 1813, when the 'First Essay on the Formation of Character' was published, but he soon encountered opposition to his views and his attempts to put them into practice at New Lanark. He therefore called a series of meetings at the London Tavern in 1817, at which he tried to give further publicity to his ideas.

It may now be asked, "If the new arrangements proposed really possess all the advantages that have been stated, why have they not been adopted in universal practice during all the ages which have passed?"

"Why should so many countless millions of our fellow-creatures, through each successive generation, have been the victims of ignorance, of superstition, of mental degradation, and of wretchedness?"

Then, my friends, I tell you, that hitherto you have been prevented from even knowing what happiness really is, solely in consequence of the errors—gross errors—that have been combined with the fundamental notions of every religion that has hitherto been taught to men. And, in consequence, they have made man the most inconsistent, and the most miserable being in existence. By the errors of these systems he has been made a weak, imbecile animal; a furious bigot and fanatic; or a miserable hypocrite; and should these qualities be carried, not only into the projected villages, but *into Paradise itself, a Paradise would be no longer found!*

From Robert Owen, *Address Delivered at the City of London Tavern on Thursday, August 21st, and published in the London Newspapers of 22 August* 1817, reprinted in (**90**), *Supplementary Appendix*, vol. IA, 1858, p. 115.

Determinism

Owenism emphasised that man is the creature of circumstances, and that his will was not free, but the product of natural motive. This theory, which was common among the philosophers of the Enlightenment, contradicted the basic teachings of Christianity. The following is from the textbook of Owen's ideas which was used by the lecturers in the Halls of Science.

How opposed are the harmony and unity of this science, to all the religions and codes of laws invented by the past generations of men, while ignorant of their own organization, and of the laws of Nature! All human laws are opposed to Nature's laws, and, therefore, discordant, disunited and perplexed, and always produce more evil than good.

The Religions founded under the name of Jewish, Budh, Jehovah, God or Christ, Mahomet or any other, are all composed of human laws in opposition to Nature's eternal laws; and when these laws are analysed, they amount only to three absurdities,—three gross impositions upon the ignorance or inexperience of mankind;—three errors, now, easily to be detected by the most simple experiment of each individual upon himself. The fundamental doctrines or laws of all these religions are, first,—*Believe in my doctrines, as expounded by my Priests, from my sacred books*; second, *Feel as these doctrines, thus expounded, direct you to feel*; and third, *Support my Ministers for thus instructing you.* "If you faithfully perform these three things in my name,"—say the Priests of all these religions—"you will have the greatest merit in this world, and an everlasting reward in the next."

All religions and all codes of laws are built on the preceding dogmas, and all presuppose the original power in man to believe and to feel as he likes.

Now the facts and laws of nature, which constitute the Moral Science of Man, demonstrate that all belief or mental convictions, and all physical feelings, are instincts of human nature, and form the will; it follows that the three fundamental dogmas of all religions have emanated from ignorance of the organization of man, and of the general laws of nature: hence the confusion in all human affairs; the inutility of all human laws, and the irrational and miserable condition of all human society.

It follows, that as all religions and codes of laws are founded in the error, that there is merit or demerit in belief and in feeling,—religions and laws must have originated in some error of the imagination, similar to the universal error, maintained through unnumbered ages, that the earth was flat, immoveable, and the centre of the universe.

But unity and harmony could never be found in any religion or codes of laws, founded on the mistaken notion that instincts were free-will, while all facts prove that the will of man is the necessary result of the action of those instincts.

From Robert Owen, *The Book of the New Moral World, containing the Rational System of Society founded on demonstrable facts, developing the Constitution and Laws of Human Nature and of Society*, London, 1836, pp. 94–5.

document 16
Immoral Socialism

Christian ministers were horrified by these ideas of Socialism, but the opponents of the new moral world greatly exaggerated its immoral implications. When the editor of the 'Gateshead Observer' made some favourable comments about the Owenites, a local Methodist minister rushed into print to disabuse the people of any friendly ideas they might entertain towards Owen's schemes.

I must say, that of all men on earth, the Socialists should be the last to make pretensions to philanthropy, or to a desire to improve the condition of society. The whole of their writings are aimed at the overthrow of society, and all their proceedings are in opposition to every principle on which society is founded. They openly profess that their intentions are to do away with all religions, to abolish all existing arrangements and institutions of society, to do away with marriage, to destroy all single family arrangements, to have property, women, and children thrown into one common stock, and to live and herd together like the beasts of the field.

From Joseph Barker, *The Abominations of Socialism Exposed, in reply to the Gateshead Observer*, Newcastle, 1840, p. 3.

A Socialist ceremony

Christianity's most powerful ally against the Socialists was the Bishop of Exeter, who, on 4 February 1840, moved in the House of Lords 'that an humble Address be presented to Her Majesty, praying that her Majesty would be pleased to command, that inquiries should be made into the diffusion of blasphemous and immoral publications, especially as to the tenets and proceedings of a society established under the name of Socialists'. He used information supplied by a number of Christian correspondents, and the following is the account he gives of a report by Brindley and Tomkins who attended one of the Sunday afternoon 'services' at the Queenwood Community.

The proceedings commenced with their 10th hymn, sung to a sacred tune—a parody on one of the hymns of the church service. Mr. Finch then read, as is usual with them on the Sunday, what they call a portion of Scripture. Could not tell what book he pretended to quote; but it was to the disparagement of Christianity, showing how little it had progressed compared with the various heathen systems. Another hymn was then sung, the 32nd in their book, to a sacred tune. The lecture was next given. He said he would take for his text that portion of what was called the Gospel which declared 'He that believeth and is baptised, shall be saved, but he that believeth not, shall be damned.' Gospel signified good news, glad tidings. He would show that the Gospel of the New Testament contained the worst news for man that could be brought him. It represented God as taking delight in damning men throughout eternity, as roasting and frizzling them alive in hell for ever. He was a fierce and cruel God. It spoke also of a devil; but did they believe such nonsense? Did they ever see a devil, or smell a devil, or chew a devil? Then it also told them of a heaven, where the few that reached it were to be engaged in singing and shouting, and falling on their faces and blowing trumpets throughout eternity, who would want such a heaven as that? He (Finch) believed the whole thing was a fiction. Socialism the only true gospel and he that believes this gospel will be saved from all future want, and care, and toil. The Gospel of the Christians was a mock Gospel. He said much to excite them against their employers and persons of property. Told them, 'They produced all the things which those persons consumed:' that 'they were kept in pining, want, and wretchedness, while the others were rolling in wealth, and living in idleness.' He again referred to the Bible, spoke of David with many obscene expressions, and then ridiculed the psalms which, 'that hypocrite wrote': said 'the Bible was a most filthy and immoral book'; that 'for one God saved, it told them the devil damned twenty'. 'He could not believe in a God damning us for what he had made us to do and be.'

From *Hansard*, li, 1840, col. 1187.

document 18

The Manchester Hall of Science

A more favourable view of what the Socialists were actually like in practice is given in a contemporary account of Manchester in 1844. A long footnote was added to the section on religion, in which the Chartist and Owenite 'services' were described.

As closely connected with the state of religion in Manchester, we may mention "Carpenter's Hall", and the "Hall of Science". The first is the Sunday resort of the Chartists. They open and close their meetings with the singing of democratic hymns, and their sermons are political discourses on the justice of democracy and the necessity for obtaining the charter. The second is an immense building in the Camp Field, raised exclusively by the savings of the mechanics and artisans, at a cost of £7,000, and which contains a lecture-hall—the finest and most spacious in the town. It is tenanted by the disciples of Mr. Owen. In addition to Sunday lectures upon the doctrines of Socialism, they possess a day and Sunday-school, and increase the number of their adherents by oratorios and festivals—by rural excursions, and by providing cheap and innocent recreation for the working classes. Their speculative doctrines aim at the destruction of all belief in revealed religion, and the establishment of community of property; and they are vigorously opposed by the evangelical portion of the religious public. It is, at the same time admitted, that they have done much to refine the habits of the working classes. They are mostly advocates of temperance societies, and never allow fermented liquors to be drunk at any of their festivals. They were among the first to introduce tea-parties at a low rate of admission; and the popularity they have obtained by these endeavours to improve the habits of their fellow-townsmen, is one great cause of their success in the propagation of their system. The large sums of money they raise, proves that they belong to the wealthier portion of the working classes. Their audiences on Sunday evenings are generally crowded.

A translator's footnote in *Manchester in 1844; its present condition and future prospects, by M. Leon Faucher, translated from the French, with copious notes appended, by a Member of the Manchester Athenaeum*, London and Manchester, 1844, p. 25.

An Atheist's view of the Bible

*The freethinking radicals attacked the Bible as the basis on which the
superstitious system of religion was erected. The more extreme writers
were none too polite in the words of criticism which they used. The
following article, contemptuously headed 'The "Jew Book"', was the
cause of Charles Southwell's prosecution for blasphemy in 1841.*

That revoltingly odious Jew production, called BIBLE, has been
for ages the idol of all sorts of blockheads, the glory of knaves,
and the disgust of wise men. It is a history of lust, sodomies,
wholesale slaughtering, and horrible depravity, that the vilest
parts of all other histories, collected into one monstrous book,
could scarcely parallel! Priests tell us that this concentration of
abominations was written by a god; all the world believe
priests, or they would rather have thought it the outpourings of
some devil!

As in these times even Atheists may write without fear of
being *roasted*, we will briefly expose this choice *morceau*. To our
minds the bible is one of the most contemptible and brutalizing
books that ever was penned! From Genesis to Revelations we
have one string of blunders. Its heroines are strumpets, an
account of whose debaucheries is fit only for the hell of human
imagination; assassinating Jezebels, the tale of whose lewdness
and infamy would put Fanny Hill or Harriet Wilson to the
blush. It is a book which contains passages so outrageously
disgusting and scandalously indecent, that were it not called
the word of a god, no modest woman would suffer it to be read
in her house. Its heroes are cruel, unscrupulous, and (from
Moses, the king of the conjurors [*sic*], to Peter and Paul, the last
of the gang)—canting, impudent impostors; slaughtering fanatics, plundering judges, and abominable kings, who if they were
to start from their graves and play their villainous pranks in
these times, would be strung up to the first lamp-post. The
prophets were impudent mouthers, who vomited forth their
sublime balderdash, prophesying and humbugging, with a
shameful disregard to personal covering, that would be deemed
scandalous among decent people; frantic bedlamites, that the

Jews, had they not been senseless idiots, would have fastened in the stocks or clapped in a pillory.

From Charles Southwell, 'The "Jew Book"', *Oracle of Reason*, no. 4, 27 November 1841.

document 20

Rationalism

As Owenism was declining, G. J. Holyoake tried to rescue its doctrines and to put them forward as the basis of a new movement. His first exposition of his principles, entitled 'Rationalism', is little more than a summary of Owen's 'Book of the New Moral World' [**doc. 15**].

RELIGION.—Rationalism invalidates many of the popular tenets of the day, and some deductions from its first principle are *hard* to be reconciled with religion, and this circumstance, more than the novelty of its political economy, has retarded its progress in society. It is necessarily discourteous to popular error. Drivelling pusillanimity would it be for rationalists to ask their neighbours whether they are to profess this creed or that, or believe or not in God. The writer takes Rationalism to be the science of *material* circumstances. Rationalism advises what is useful to society without asking whether it is religious or not. It makes morality the sole business of life, and declares that from the cradle to the grave man should be guided by reason and regulated by science. It looks on man, to all practical purposes, as a purely material being—other systems have chiefly spiritualised him. It would have been well if they had spiritualised his miseries, but they have only refined into nothings his happiness, and left his wrongs and wretchedness solid, material, and enduring. Rationalism does not regard man through the distorting spectacles of theology, which reveals only wounds, bruises, and putrifying [*sic*] sores, but discovers in humanity the germs of indefinite moral progression, which the genial influences of truth, love, and justice will develope [*sic*], and intelligence nourish for ever.

From G. J. Holyoake, *Rationalism, a Treatise for the Times*, London, 1845, pp. 30–1.

Secular principles

In the 1850s, Holyoake developed out of Rationalism a system which he entitled Secularism. This he defined in moderate language, not as Atheism, but as a philosophy which sought to promote secular improvement by avoiding theological controversy. His interpretation of Secularism was widely accepted, and the following is taken from a leaflet printed in Rochdale.

1. Secularism is a name given to a series of principles of Positivism, intended for the guidance of those who find Theology indefinite, or inadequate, or deem it unreliable.
2. A Secularist is one who gives special attention to those speculations the issues of which can be tested by the experience of this life.
3. Secularism seeks to discern what *is* in Nature; studies what ought to be in morals, and selects the affirmative in exposition. It concerns itself with the *real*, the *right*, and the *constructive*.
4. Its moral basis is, that justification by sincerity is a higher and nobler truth than justification by faith.
5. Its province of study is the order rather than the origin of Nature, the study of the laws or operations of Nature being the most fruitful for human guidance.
6. Its theory of morals: that there exist guarantees of pure morality in human nature—utility, experience, and intelligence; that conduct is the true source of acceptability; that human service is the noblest prayer, and work the highest *worship*.
7. Secularism teaches that science is the available providence of man.
8. Secularism teaches that conscience is higher than consequences.
9. Secularism teaches that the methods of mind are as uniform and as calculable as the methods of nature, and that whoever masters the process of human affairs may come to control the results.
10. Secularism teaches that human nature is improvable under well-understood conditions.
11. Secularism teaches that the dependence or the well-being

of one depends upon that of all; that care for others is a matter of well-understood self-defence.

12. Secularism teaches the moral innocence of all sincere opinion; that sincerity, though not errorless, involves the least chance of error, and is without moral guilt.

From *Secular Principles*, a leaflet in the Holyoake Collection, (2), no. 4346.

document 22

A Secularist meeting, 1874

The Secularists and other ultra-radical groups usually met in back-street halls (though see **doc. 18** *for contrast). The Reverend C. M. Davies made a hobby of visiting the more unusual groups on Sunday evenings, and his albeit frivolous reports are among the best records of what these meetings were like.*

Sunday evening is the only chance you have got of catching Heterodoxy in full swing; so that it would take a slice out of a lifetime to do more than focus a few forms of Proteus. This fact, and a very imperfect system of advertisement on the part of our heretics, must be my excuse if I omit any "representative men." So it was that I set off with my *alter ego* for Moorgate Street, whence, I found, the tramway cars would set me down at the Hall of Perseverance and the shrine of the Hackney Athene respectively.

Out of Goldsmith's Row, which is slummy, just past the almshouses, turns a court which is slummier still; and Perseverance Hall is slummiest of all. There is no outward sign or symbol of the Temple of Perseverance, and you have to grub your way into a most unlikely-looking doorway; but we went in. We would have gone into anything that stood open, for we had long been pacing Goldsmith's Row infructuously in the drizzle of a March evening. Nobody knew where Perseverance Hall was, but everybody told us; so no wonder we wandered. Chance, however, at last guided us; and as we pushed open the refractory little doors we found ourselves in a small lecture-hall, with the customary paraphernalia of platform and baized table at the farther end. An old gentleman, sitting with his hat on in the front seat, might have been the personification of Perseverance under its aspect of Punctuality; for he told us that there was a good hour to wait yet before the Biblical Heroes would come on for annihilation.

The first thing I noticed was that the room smelt. I suspect drains; but I know it was nasty—stuffy is, I believe, the correct expression. The people, too, seemed of a lower order than those with whom I had hitherto been brought into contact. There were a few tidy working-men; but with a good many of the gathering the close connexion of cleanliness with godliness had been so practically recognised, that they abjured the former with the latter.

By-and-by time was called; the youthful chairman assumed his place, looking as much like Nestor as he could, and the lecturer, an elderly, pleasant-faced man stood on his left at the table. There were, I should think, about thirty men and one woman present when he commenced. The male audience was increased gradually during the lecture; but the female, who looked like a decent domestic servant, remained in her minority of one.

From the Reverend Charles Maurice Davies, 'Hackney propagandism', in *Heterodox London: or, Phases of Free Thought in the Metropolis*, 2 vols, London, 1874, i, 252–3, 255.

document 23

A freethought hymn

The freethinkers held 'services' at which they sang secular hymns (see **docs 17, 18***). A copy of one such hymn is written on a sheet of letter paper, headed the Land Reform Association, of New York, and was probably used by Holyoake when he visited America in either 1879 or 1882.*

Hymn 1

Religion, a delusion and curse,
By Lewis Masquerier

Tune—'Battle cry of Freedom'

120

We are rousing for free speaking, to censure or applaud,
  And claim the sceptic's right to reason.
We must disbelieve all dogmas, the spawn of priest and god,
  That curse mankind with crime and folly.

Chorus—Free speech man's redeemer, arouse sceptics, rouse:
      Blot out all bibles—dare speak the truth:
      We are humanizing christians, we wean them from
        their gods,
      And give them better sense and morals.

2.
We free thinkers should be honored and pensioned by
    the church,*
  For having stopped its cruel warfare:
Having snatched the christian's faggot from his fanatic clutch,
  And stopped the burning of each other.

Chorus—Free speech, &c.

3.
Oh, in vain has priestcraft striven to sever mind from brain,
  And strove to build a world with spirits.
Mind, no more than life or motion, can never live again,
  But dies forever with its organs.

Chorus—Free speech, &c.

4.
Priests declare mankind are hell-bent, as being born depraved,
  Are Satan's convicts till Christ pardoned.
But it is a stupid slander, that they are lost or saved,
  Can be *white-washed* with blood of Jesus.

Chorus—Free speech, &c.

5.
But men's virtues and their vices engender by degrees,
  And grow by habits oft repeated;
If well organized and balanced in all their faculties,
  Right practice ever gives them virtue.

Chorus—Free speech, &c.

From Holyoake Collection (2), no. 4340.

  * Supposing the principle of a pension was correct.

VI. RADICAL REPUBLICANISM

document 24

Chartism and infidelity

The British radical movement was divided into several different and distinct organisations, of which Chartism was only one. When the Reverend Dr John Campbell tried to equate Chartism with the infidel radicals in the Congregationalist periodical, the 'British Banner', G. J. Harney wrote an angry reply in the 'Northern Star', although he himself was both a Chartist and an Infidel.

In plain English, Dr. Campbell, you assert that which is false. There is nothing concerning Infidelity in the Charter. That document is thoroughly a political measure, taking no account of men's creeds—of their belief or disbelief. The Charter recognises neither Christian nor Jew, neither believer nor Infidel, neither Protestant nor Catholic. The Charter proposes to confer upon all men of mature age, sound mind, and not under punishment for crime, the rights of citizenship—or, rather, the power to exercise those rights which are the natural and inalienable property of all.

But Holyoake, Owen, and Southwell are not Chartists. Carlile, Taylor, Mirabeau [*sic*], and Diderot were not Chartists. True, the great man whom you insolently term 'Tom Paine' first popularised those democratic principles on which Chartism is based; but his 'Rights of Man,' and his 'Age of Reason,' are works thoroughly distinct. Chartism recognises the principles of the former, but leaves every man to judge for himself of the latter. Chartism has no more connection with 'Paine's theological works' than it has with the canting trash of the editor of the *Banner*.

Reprinted in *Reasoner*, iv, no. 91, 23 February 1848, pp. 180–1.

Freedom of the individual

The political creed of the Secularists was that expressed in J. S. Mill's 'Essay on Liberty', which advocated freedom from all restraint on the individual so that men could develop as moral beings independently of any State interference. This point of view was strongly urged by Holyoake in his debate on compulsory Total Abstinence with F. R. Lees, the leading advocate of the Temperance Movement.

Between the advocates of Sabbath restriction and Maine-laws, there will soon be neither liberty nor enjoyment left to the poor-man. . . . Force is a present evil. It is saving drunkards and making tyrants. Even good forced upon another is evil to him.

"*The world is too much governed.*" Laws are the expedients of governments that, not knowing the conditions of nature, are obliged to substitute those of art and force. It is bad enough when *Governments* impose coercive regulations—it is worse when the people ask for them in order to subjugate each other. America, the land of extremes, is no model for us. You invoke a Maine-law against the drunkard, because he cannot, *you say*, take care of himself. Slavery is a Maine-law against liberty—because Slaveholders think the Negro cannot take care of himself. Rome seeks to put down the Bible on the Maine-law principle; and declares Protestantism to be a poison, which the weak and ignorant take. The worst you can say of Alcohol is, that it inflames the bad passions of a man, but the Vegetarians, with great show of reason, allege that the diet of blood and flesh engenders new passions in a man. Over every Publican's door the Teetotaller would write 'CRIME'—over every Butcher's door the Vegetarian would write 'DISEASE.'

. . . The difference between Dr. Lees and myself is not so much in the object, as that he does not realise *the evil of the method*—a method that may be invoked for many evil purposes. Transport the drunkard if you will—but do not coerce the sober.

From the *Discussion at Derby* between G. J. Holyoake and F. R. Lees, London, 1856, printed in *The Works of F. R. Lees*, pp. cxci, cc.

Objects of the National Secular Society

The National Secular Society was more than an organisation opposed to religion: it espoused the whole radical programme of attacks on the privileged groups of Church, landlords and aristocracy. The sixth point, however, shows that the Secularists were committed to the middle-class faith in Political Economy.

The Executive of the National Secular Society, finding that the power of the Freethought body in the State is specially recognised in connection with the political and social changes now taking place, points out to its members and friends the following matters as deserving of their earnest and active attention:—

1. To obtain the repeal of the Blasphemy Laws as a special matter affecting its members.

2. The disestablishment and disendowment of the State Church, and the placing of all religions and forms of speculative opinion on a perfect equality before the law.

3. Specially the improvement of the condition of the Agricultural classes, whose terrible state of social degradation is at present a fatal barrier to the formation of good state of society.

4. A change in the Land Laws, so as to break down the present system by which enormous estates are found in few hands, the many having no interest in the soil, and to secure for the Agricultural labourer some share of the improvement in the land he cultivates.

5. The destruction of the present hereditary Chamber of Peers, and substitution of a Senate containing Life Members, elected for their fitness, and therewith the constitution of a National Party intended to wrest the governing power from a few Whig and Tory families.

6. The investigation of the causes of poverty in all old countries, in order to see how far unequal distribution of wealth or more radical causes may operate. The discussion in connection with this of the various schemes for social amelioration, and the ascertainment if possible of the laws governing the increase of population and produce, as affecting the rise and fall of wages.

From *The Secularist's Manual of Songs and Ceremonies* [1870], (2), p. 6.

The attack on the Queen

The main objects of the Republican attack were the Queen and the aristocracy. In two of his most influential works, Bradlaugh condemned them both.

For many years her Majesty has taken but little part in the show ceremonials of State. Parliament is usually opened and closed by commission—a robe on an empty throne, and a speech read by deputy, satisfying the Sovereign's loyal subjects. It is, however, the fact that in real State policy her interference has been most mischievous, and this especially where it affected her Prusso-German relatives. In the case of Denmark attacked by Prussia and Austria, and in the case of the Franco-Prussian War, English Court influences have most indecently affected our foreign relations.

Her Majesty is now enormously rich, and—as she is like her Royal grandmother—grows richer daily. She is also generous, and has recently given not quite half a day's income to the starving poor of India. A few months prior to this many thousands of pounds were wasted in formally proclaiming her imperial.

From C. Bradlaugh, *The Impeachment of the House of Brunswick*, 6th edn, London, 1880, p. 99.

The attack on the aristocracy

The enormous estates of the few landed proprietors must not only be prevented from growing larger, they must be broken up. At their own instance and gradually, if they will meet us with even a semblance of fairness, for the poor and hungry cannot well afford to fight; but at our instance, and rapidly, if they obstinately refuse all legislation. If they will not commence inside the House of Parliament, then from the outside we must make them listen. If they claim that in this we are unfair, our answer is ready—

You have monopolised the land, and while you have got each year a wider and firmer grip, you have cast its burdens on others; you have made labour pay the taxes which land could more easily have borne. You now claim that the rights of property in land should be respected, while you have too frequently by your settlements and entails kept your lands out of the possibility of fulfilling any of the obligations of property, and you have robbed your tradespeople and creditors, because your land was protected by cunningly contrived statutes and parchments against all duty, while it enjoyed all privilege. You have been intolerant in your power, driving your tenants to the poll like cattle, keeping your labourers ignorant and demoralised, and yet charging them with this very ignorance and degradation as an incapacity for the enjoyment of political rights. For the last quarter of a century, by a short-sighted policy, and in order to diminish your poor-rates, you have demolished the cottages on your estates, compelling the wretched agricultural labourers, whose toils gave value to your land, to crowd into huts even more foul and dilapidated than those you destroyed. We no longer pray, we argue—we no longer entreat, we insist—that spade and plough, and sickle and scythe, shall have fair right to win life and happiness for our starving from the land which gave us birth.

From C. Bradlaugh, *The Land, the People, and the Coming Struggle*, 3rd edn, London, 1877, p. 15.

The case for Socialism

In April 1884 Charles Bradlaugh, the champion of individualism and radicalism, debated Socialism with the leader of the S.D.F., the Marxist H. M. Hyndman. Their two points of view illustrate the contrast between the old Liberalism and the new Socialism. Hyndman argued the case of the poor, oppressed by the middle class; Bradlaugh repeated the need for freedom which had earlier been put by Holyoake [doc. 25].

HYNDMAN

Now then, first and foremost, men are born into this world, hundreds and thousands of them, without any property whatsoever—(Oh, oh)—or any claim to any property. We are all born without any property. They arrive at manhood and womanhood in that condition—thousands of them. What is their position? They have no property, no command over the means of production, either land, capital, machinery, or credit, either as individuals or as part of the organised community. Under what conditions, then, have they to live? They have not one thing which they possess but the force of labor in their bodies. Mind, what I am saying applies not only to the worker, not only to the distributor who is working on the railways, &c., but it applies in a very large degree to the small shopkeepers and clerks and those who live by intellectual labor. They have to compete against one another in what is called the labor market in order to be able only to exist. Under what circumstances do they so compete? The middle class economists all tell us that the law of that competition is that they get on the average the standard of life in the country in which they were born, and just so much as will enable them to hand on the same lot to their successors. There are some who get more; there are some highly skilled laborers who receive more than this, but there are others, as some perhaps here may well know, who for months never get a full meal, and there are whole classes who, as the official reports tell us, never get enough food to keep them clear of the diseases which arise from starvation.

From H. M. Hyndman and C. Bradlaugh, *Will Socialism Benefit the English People?*, London, 1884, pp. 5–6.

The case for Liberalism and Secularism

BRADLAUGH
What is a property-owner? A property-owner is that person who
has anything whatever beyond what is necessary for the actual
existence of the moment. All savings in the Savings Bank,
the Co-operative Store, the Building Society, the Friendly
Society and the Assurance Society are property; and I will show
you that there are millions of working men in this country who
are in that condition. (Applause.) It is not true that the majority
are starving. ... Property-owners belong to all classes—the
wage-earning class are largely property-owners. (Oh, oh, and
laughter.) ... I object that in a Socialistic State there would be
no inducement to thrift, no individual savings, no accumulation, no check upon waste. I say that on the contrary you
would have paralysis and neutralisation of endeavor, and that
in fact you would simply go back, you could not go forward.
(Hear, hear.) I urge that the only sufficient inducement to the
general urging on of progress in society is by individual effort,
spurred to action by the hope of private gain; it may be gain of
money, it may be gain in other kind, it may be gain in the
praise of fellows or sharing their greater happiness; but whatever it is, it is the individual motive which prompts and spurs
the individual to action. (Hear, hear.) In this Collective
Socialism, the State would direct everything, and there could
be no freedom of opinion at all except that which the State
ordered and directed. (Rubbish.)

From *ibid.*, pp. 16, 17–18.

Socialism and unbelief

*Men of all kinds of religious and antireligious views joined the Socialist
Movement. Robert Blatchford, the editor of the 'Clarion', was a violent
opponent of Christianity, and used many of the same arguments as had
Robert Cooper half a century earlier [see* doc. 2*].*

Holiness! Your religion does not make it.—Its ethics are too weak, its theories too unsound, its transcendentalism is too thin. Take as an example this much admired passage from St. James:

> Pure religion and undefiled is this before God and the Father, to visit the fatherless and widows in their affliction, and to keep oneself unspotted from the world.

The widows and the fatherless are our brothers and sisters and our flesh and blood, and should be at home in our hearts and on our hearths. And who that is a man will work to keep himself unspotted from the world if the service of the world needs him to expose his flesh and his soul to risk?

I can fancy a Reverend Gentleman going to Heaven, unspotted from the world, to face the awful eyes of a Heavenly Father whose gaze has been on London.

A good man mixes with the world in the rough-and-tumble; and takes his share of the dangers, and the falls, and the temptations. His duty is to work and to help, and not to shirk and keep his hands white. His business is not to be holy, but to be useful.

In such a world as this, friend Christian, a man has no business reading the Bible, singing hymns, and attending divine worship. He has not *time*. All the strength and pluck and wit he possesses are needed in the work of real religion, of real salvation. The rest is all "dreams out of the ivory gate, and visions before midnight."

There ought to be no such thing as poverty in the world. The earth is bounteous: the ingenuity of man is great. He who defends the claims of the individual, or of a class, against the rights of the human race is a criminal.

A hungry man, an idle man, an ignorant man, a destitute or degraded woman, a beggar or pauper child is a reproach to Society and a witness against existing religion and civilisation.

From Robert Blatchford, *God and my Neighbour*, London, 1903, p. 194.

Socialism and Christianity

Christian influences were strong in the idealism of the Socialist Movement. In contrast to Blatchford, Keir Hardie saw pure Christianity as a powerful support to Socialism.

The Sermon on the Mount, whilst it perhaps lends but small countenance to State Socialism, is full of the spirit of pure Communism. Nay, in its lofty contempt for thrift and forethought, it goes far in advance of anything ever put forward by any Communist, ancient or modern. Christ's denunciations of wealth are only equalled by the fierceness of the diatribes which He levelled against the Pharisees. It was St. Paul who enunciated the doctrine that he who would not work neither should he eat, whilst St. James in his Epistle rivals the old prophets in his treatment of those who grow rich at the expense of the poor. Contrary to the generally accepted opinion, it is now known that Communism in goods was practised by Christians for at least three hundred years after the death of Christ. Almost without exception, the early Christian Fathers whose teachings have come down to us spoke out fearlessly against usury, which includes interest also, and on the side of Communism. They proclaimed that, inasmuch as nature had provided all things in common, it was sinful robbery for one man to own more than another, especially if that other was in want. The man who gathered much whilst others had not enough, was a murderer. The poor had a right to their share of everything there was, which is different from the charity so common nowadays. If a man inherited wealth he was, if not a robber himself, but the recipient of stolen goods, since no accumulation of wealth could be come by honestly. To those who said that the idleness of the poor was the cause of their poverty, St. John Chrysostom replied that the rich too were idlers living on their plunder.

From J. Keir Hardie, *From Serfdom to Socialism*, London, 1907, pp. 38–40.

Christian Socialism

Some Christians responded to the arguments of the Socialists. In the mid-nineteenth century, the followers of F. D. Maurice had been 'Christian Socialist' by name, although they did not attack private property. Towards the end of the century, a new school of Christian Socialists was much more extreme. Its leader was the Reverend Stewart D. Headlam. The following is from a Fabian Socialist tract by him.

I take it that we are all agreed that, under the best Socialist *régime* imaginable, if a man is a loafer, whether of the east or west, if a man refuse to work when he has every facility and opportunity for working, he will fall into poverty or into something much more disagreeable than poverty. But what is it we see now? Why, this: that on the whole those who work the hardest and produce the most have the least of the good things of this world for their consumption; and those who work very little and produce nothing, or nothing adequate in return for what they consume, have the most of the good things of this world for their consumption. So much so, that, as we have been taught, all society at present can be classified into beggars, robbers, and workers. If a man is not working for his living, he must either be a beggar, living on the charity of others, or a robber preying upon the hard-won earnings of others. And if, again, you want a rough description of the object of Christian Socialism, I should say that it was to bring about the time when all shall work, and when, all working, work will be a joy instead of the "grind" it is at present, and to bring about the time when the robbers shall be utterly abolished.

From S. D. Headlam, *Socialism and Religion*, London, 1908, pp. 11–12.

Bibliography

This study is based partly on the works listed in the bibliography, and partly on pamphlets too numerous and obscure to be individually mentioned below. Excellent collections of such primary sources can be found in almost any large city reference library, Birmingham, Leeds, Leicester, Manchester and Newcastle upon Tyne being particularly good. In London, apart from the British Museum, the Bishopsgate Institute and the National Secular Society are rich in source materials.

MANUSCRIPTS

1   Robert Owen Papers, Co-operative Union, Manchester.
2   George Jacob Holyoake Papers, Co-operative Union, Manchester.
3   George Jacob Holyoake Papers, Bishopsgate Institute, London.
4   Joseph Cowen, jnr, Papers, Newcastle upon Tyne Public Library.

PERIODICALS

5   *Republican* (Richard Carlile, 1819–26).
6   *New Moral World* (G. A. Fleming, 1834–45).
7   *Oracle of Reason* (Charles Southwell, 1841–43).
8   *Movement* (G. J. Holyoake, 1843–45).
9   *Reasoner* (G. J. Holyoake, 1846–61).
10   *Investigator* (R. Cooper, 1854–59).
11   *National Reformer* (Charles Bradlaugh, 1860–93).

REPORTS AND ANNUALS

12   *Annual Register, passim*
13   *Hansard, passim*.

14 *Minutes of the Committee of Council on Education*, H.M.S.O., 1846.
15 *Annual Reports* of the Manchester and Salford Town Missionary Society (Evangelical), 1838–62.
16 *Annual Reports* of the Ministry to the Poor (Unitarian), Manchester, 1837–61; Leicester, 1846–62.

PRINTED COLLECTIONS OF SOURCES

17 Cole, G. D. H. and Filson, A. W. *British Working Class Movements*, Macmillan, 1965.
18 Hanham, H. J. *The Nineteenth-Century Constitution 1815–1914*, Cambridge University Press, 1969.
19 Maclure, J. S. *Educational Documents, England and Wales, 1816–1967*, 2nd edn, Chapman & Hall, 1968.
20 Pelling, H. *The Challenge of Socialism*, 2nd edn, A. and C. Black, 1968.

GENERAL READING

21 Cole, G. D. H. *A Short History of the British Working Class Movement*, Allen & Unwin, 1948: the best general introduction to radical history.
22 Maccoby, S. *English Radicalism*, 6 vols, Allen & Unwin, 1935–61.
23 Derry, J. W. *The Radical Tradition*, Macmillan, 1967.
24 Webb, S. and Webb, B. *The History of Trade Unionism*, Longmans, 1920.
25 Hobsbawm, E. J. *Primitive Rebels*, Manchester University Press, 1959.
26 Hobsbawm, E. J. *Labouring Men*, Weidenfeld & Nicolson, 1964.

INTELLECTUAL HISTORY

27 Stephen, L. *History of English Thought in the Eighteenth Century*, 2 vols, 3rd edn, Smith, Elder, 1902.
28 Robertson, J. M. *A History of Freethought in the Nineteenth Century*, Watts, 1929.
29 Gillispie, C. C. *Genesis and Geology*, Harvard University Press, 1951.

30 Halévy, E. *The Growth of Philosophical Radicalism*, trans. M. Morris, Faber, 1929: the best introduction to intellectual currents at the end of the eighteenth century.

31 Houghton, W. E. *The Victorian Frame of Mind, 1830–1870*, Yale University Press, 1957.

32 Cockshut, A. O. J. *The Unbelievers: English agnostic thought 1840–1890*, Collins, 1964.

33 Willey, B. *More Nineteenth Century Studies. A group of honest doubters*, Chatto & Windus, 1956.

LITERACY AND EDUCATION

34 Webb, R. K. *The British Working Class Reader, 1790–1848. Literacy and social tension*, Allen & Unwin, 1955: an excellent study.

35 Altick, R. D. *The English Common Reader*, Chicago University Press, 1957.

36 Simon, B. *Studies in the History of Education, 1780–1870*, Lawrence & Wishart, 1960: the best outline of education and radicalism.

37 Harrison, J. F. C. *Learning and Living. A study of the history of the English Adult Education Movement*, Routledge & Kegan Paul, 1961.

38 Stone, L. 'Literacy and Education in England, 1640–1900', *Past and Present*, no. 42, Feb. 1969, pp. 69–139.

RELIGION

Sources

39 Mann, H. *Census of Great Britain, 1851. Religious worship in England and Wales, abridged from the official report . . .* , Routledge, 1854.

40 Mudie-Smith, R., ed. *The Religious Life of London*, Hodder & Stoughton, 1904.

Secondary reading

41 Chadwick W. O. *The Victorian Church*, 2 vols, A. and C. Black, 1966–70.

42 Inglis, K. S. *Churches and the Working Classes in Victorian England*, Routledge & Kegan Paul, 1963.

Together, nos. **41** and **42** provide the best introduction to nineteenth-century religious history.

43 Taylor, E. R. *Methodism and Politics, 1791–1851*, Cambridge University Press, 1935.

44 Wearmouth, R. F. (**a**) *Methodism and the Working Class Movements of England, 1800–50*, Epworth, 1937; and (**b**) *Methodism and the Struggle of the Working Classes, 1850–1900*, Leicester, Edgar Backus, 1954.

45 Currie, R. B. *Methodism Divided*, Faber, 1969.

46 Davies, E. T. *Religion in the Industrial Revolution in South Wales*, University of Wales Press, 1965.

47 Faulkner, H. U. *Chartism and the Churches* (Columbia University: *Studies in History, Economics, &c.*, vol. 73, no. 3), New York, 1916; reprinted by Frank Cass, 1970.

48 Wickham, E. R. *Church and People in an Industrial City*, Lutterworth, 1957: a pioneer local study of Sheffield.

49 Inglis, K. S. 'Patterns of worship in 1851', *Journal of Ecclesiastical History*, xi, 1960, pp. 74–86.

50 Thompson, D. M. 'The 1851 Religious Census', *Victorian Studies*, xi, no. 1, Sept. 1967, pp. 87–97.

51 Raven, C. E. *Christian Socialism, 1848–54*, Macmillan, 1920.

52 Christensen, T. *The Origin and History of Christian Socialism, 1848–54 (Acta Theologica Danica*, vol. iii), Universitetsforlaget i Aarhus, 1962.

53 Mayor, S. *The Churches and the Labour Movement*, Independent Press, 1967.

54 Pelling, H. 'Popular attitudes to religion', in *Popular Politics and Society in Late Victorian Britain*, Macmillan, 1968, pp. 19–36.

55 Smith, A. 'Popular religion', *Past and Present*, no. 40, July 1968, pp. 181–6.

56 Williams, C. R. 'The Welsh religious revival, 1904–5', *British Journal of Sociology*, iii, 1953, pp. 242–59.

RADICALISM, 1789–1832

Sources

57 Reid, W. H. *The Rise and Dissolution of the Infidel Societies in this Metropolis*, J. Hatchard, 1800.

58 Paine, Thomas: the best collection of Paine's writings, and the most convenient for the *Theological Works*, is *The Complete*

Writings of Thomas Paine, ed. P. Foner, New York, Citadel Press, 1945, 2 vols. *The Rights of Man*, ed. H. Collins, Penguin, 1969, has a valuable introduction on Paine.

59 Bamford, S. *Early Days* and *Passages in the Life of a Radical*, ed. H. Dunckley, T. Fisher Unwin, 1893.

Secondary reading

60 Thompson, E. P. *The Making of the English Working Class*, Gollancz, 1965; Penguin, 1968: a brilliant and comprehensive study of the origins of the radical movement.

61 Twynam, E. *Peter Annet, 1693–1769*, Pioneer Press, [1938].

62 Conway, M. D. *The Life of Thomas Paine*, New York, Putnam, 1892, 2 vols: the pioneer work on Paine and still one of the best.

63 Aldridge, A. O. *Man of Reason. The Life of Thomas Paine*, Cresset Press, 1960.

64 Williams, G. A. *Artisans and Sans-Culottes*, Arnold, 1968.

65 Collins, H. 'The London Corresponding Society', in *Democracy and the Labour Movement*, ed. J. Saville, Lawrence & Wishart, 1954, pp. 103–34.

66 Koch, G. A. *Republican Religion. The American Revolution and the Cult of Reason*, New York, Henry Holt, 1933.

67 White, R. J. *Waterloo to Peterloo*, Heinemann, 1957; Penguin, 1968.

68 Wickwar, W. H. *The Struggle for the Freedom of the Press, 1819–1832*, Allen & Unwin, 1928: the only really adequate study of the Carlile agitation.

69 Rose, J. H. 'The unstamped press, 1815–36', *English Historical Review*, 1897, pp. 711–26.

70 Briggs, A. *Press and public in early nineteenth century Birmingham*, Dugdale Society Occasional Paper, no. 8, Oxford, 1949.

71 Henriques, U. *Religious Toleration in England, 1787–1833*, Routledge & Kegan Paul, 1961.

72 Campbell, T. C. *The Battle of the Press as told in the story of the Life of Richard Carlile, by his daughter*, A. and H. B. Bonner, 1899: principally letters of Carlile linked by a commentary.

73 Aldred, G. A. *Richard Carlile ...*, 3rd rev. edn, Glasgow, Strickland Press, 1941.

74 Cole, G. D. H. *Richard Carlile*, Fabian Society Biographical Series no. 13, Gollancz, 1943.

75 Williams, G. A. *Rowland Detrosier . . .* , Borthwick Papers no. 28, York, St Anthony's Press, 1965.

76 Barker, A. G. *Henry Hetherington, 1792–1849*, Pioneer Press, 1938.

77 Hollis, P. *The Pauper Press*, Oxford University Press, 1970: the best study of the Hetherington agitation.

78 Aldred, G. A. *The Devil's Chaplain. The story of the Rev. Robert Taylor*, Glasgow, Strickland Press, 1942.

79 Cutner, H. *Robert Taylor (1784–1844). The Devil's Chaplain*, Pioneer Press, n.d.

80 Linton, W. J. *James Watson*, Manchester, A. Heywood, 1879.

RADICALISM, 1832–85

Sources

81 Adams, W. E. *Memoirs of a Social Atom*, Hutchinson, 1903, 2 vols.

82 Barker, J. T. *The Life of Joseph Barker, written by himself, edited by his nephew*, Hodder & Stoughton, 1880.

83 Cooper, T. *The Life of Thomas Cooper*, Hodder & Stoughton, 1873.

84 Frost, T. *Forty Years' Recollections*, Sampson Low, Marston, Searle & Rivington, 1880.

85 Holyoake, G. J. *Sixty Years of an Agitator's Life*, T. Fisher Unwin, 1892, 2 vols.

86 Holyoake, G. J. *Bygones Worth Remembering*, T. Fisher Unwin, 1905, 2 vols.

87 Jones, E. *Ernest Jones, Chartist. Selections from the writings and speeches of Ernest Jones with introduction and notes*, ed. J. Saville, Lawrence & Wishart, 1952.

88 Linton, W. J. *Memories*, Lawrence & Bullen, 1895.

89 Lovett, W. *The Life and Struggles of William Lovett*, Trübner, 1876.

90 Owen, R. *The Life of Robert Owen, written by himself*, Effingham Wilson, 1857–8, 2 vols; reprinted by Frank Cass, 1967: contains Owen's own collection of his early writings; see also *A New View of Society . . .* , ed. V. A. C. Gatrell, Penguin, 1970, with a useful introduction by the editor.

Secondary reading

91 Sargant, W. L. *Robert Owen and his Social Philosophy*, Smith, Elder & Co., 1860.

92 Jones, L. *The Life, Times and Labours of Robert Owen*, 2nd edn, Swann Sonnenschein, 1895: includes a biographical note on Lloyd Jones by William Cairns Jones.

93 Podmore, F. *Robert Owen*, Allen & Unwin, 1906: still the standard work.

94 Cole, G. D. H. *Life of Robert Owen*, 3rd edn, Cass, 1965.

95 Harrison, J. F. C. *Robert Owen and the Owenites in Britain and America*, Routledge & Kegan Paul, 1969: essential reading for an understanding of Owenism and other early nineteenth-century popular movements; contains a very full bibliography of Owenite writings.

96 Cole, G. D. H. *A History of Socialist Thought*: vol. I, *The Forerunners 1789–1850*, Macmillan, 1965.

97 Silver, H. *The Concept of Popular Education*, MacGibbon & Kee, 1965: a useful study of Owenite ideas.

98 Armytage, W. H. G. *Heavens Below. Utopian experiments in England, 1560–1960*, Routledge & Kegan Paul, 1961.

99 Holyoake, G. J. *The History of Co-operation*, rev. edn, T. Fisher Unwin, 1906: a poor history but invaluable as the 'inside story' of the early co-operative movement.

100 Cole, G. D. H. *A Century of Co-operation*, Manchester, Co-operative Union, 1945: the best general history of co-operation, marred by the exigencies of wartime production.

101 Bonner, A. *British Co-operation*, Manchester, Co-operative Union, 1961: concerned mainly with twentieth-century developments; useful biographical sketches appended.

102 Hovell, M. *The Chartist Movement*, 2nd edn, Manchester University Press, 1925: still the best study of radicalism in the 1830s and the origins of the Chartist movement.

103 Cole, G. D. H. *Chartist Portraits*, rev. edn, with an Introduction by Asa Briggs, Macmillan, 1965.

104 Briggs, A., ed. *Chartist Studies*, Macmillan, 1959.

105 Mather, F. C. *Public Order in the Age of the Chartists*, Manchester University Press, 1959.

106 Dodds, J. W. *The Age of Paradox: a biography of England, 1841–51*, Gollancz, 1953: an impressionistic study with some useful insights.

107 Gillespie, F. E. *Labor and Politics in England, 1850–1867*, Duke University Press, 1927: almost the only full study of mid-century popular radicalism.

108 Briggs, A. *Victorian People*, Odhams, 1954; Penguin, 1965.

109 Harrison, R. *Before the Socialists. Studies in labour and politics 1861–1881*, Routledge & Kegan Paul, 1965: an excellent study of the Reform League, Republicanism and the Positivists.

110 Schoyen, A. R. *The Chartist Challenge*, Heinemann, 1958: a biography of G. J. Harney which extends into a history of international republicanism in the mid-nineteenth century.

111 Jones, E. R. *The Life and Speeches of Joseph Cowen, M.P.*, Sampson Low, Marston, Searle & Rivington, 1885: the best available life of this neglected republican leader.

112 Jenkins, R. *Sir Charles Dilke*, rev. edn, Collins, 1965; Fontana, 1968.

113 Collet, C. D. *History of the Taxes on Knowledge, their Origin and Repeal*, T. Fisher Unwin, 1899, 2 vols; abridged version Watts, 1933: a poor history, but with a wealth of detail about the movement.

FREETHOUGHT

Sources

114 Holyoake, G. J. *The Last Trial for Alleged Atheism in England*, 1850, 3rd edn, rev. 1861.

115 Bradlaugh, C. *Humanity's Gain from Unbelief, and other selections from the works of Charles Bradlaugh*, Watts, 1929.

116 Gilmour, J. P., ed. *Charles Bradlaugh. Champion of Liberty*, C. A. Watts, and Pioneer Press, 1933: includes selections from Bradlaugh's writings.

117 Conway, M. D. *Autobiography, Memories and Experiences*, Cassell, 1904, 2 vols.

Secondary reading

118 McGee, J. E. *A History of the British Secular Movement*, Girard, Kansas, Haldeman-Julius Publications, 1948: a work difficult to acquire in Britain, but not yet supplanted by any other study.

119 Tribe, D. *100 Years of Freethought*, Elek Books, 1967: the best general survey of modern humanism, by the President of the National Secular Society.

120 Smith, W. S. *The London Heretics, 1870–1914*, Constable, 1967.

121 Gould, F. J. *The History of the Leicester Secular Society*, Leicester, 1900.

122 Gould, F. J. *The Pioneers of Johnson's Court—history of the Rationalist Press Association from 1899 onwards*, Watts, 1929.

123 Bonner, H. B. and Robertson, J. M. *Charles Bradlaugh*, T. Fisher Unwin, 1894, 2 vols.

124 Arnstein, W. L. *The Bradlaugh Case*, Oxford University Press, 1965.

125 McCabe, J. *Life and Letters of George Jacob Holyoake*, Rationalist Press Association, and Watts, 1908, 2 vols.

126 Goss, C. W. F. *A Descriptive Bibliography of the Writings of George Jacob Holyoake, with a brief sketch of his life*, Crowther & Goodman, 1908: an almost complete guide to Holyoake's works.

127 Nethercot, A. H. *The First Five Lives of Annie Besant*, Hart-Davis, 1961.

128 Budd, S. 'The loss of faith in England, 1850–1950', *Past and Present*, no. 36, April 1967, pp. 106–25.

129 Eros, J. 'The rise of organised freethought in mid-Victorian England', *Sociological Review*, ii, no. 1, July 1954, pp. 98–120.

130 Murphy, H. R. 'The ethical revolt against Christian orthodoxy in early Victorian England', *American Historical Review*, lx, no. 4, July 1955, pp. 800–17.

131 Smith, F. B. 'The Atheist Mission, 1840–1900', in *Ideas and Institutions of Victorian Britain*, ed. R. Robson, G. Bell, 1967, pp. 205–35.

SOCIALISM
Sources

132 Blatchford, R. *My Eighty Years*, Cassell, 1931.

133 Hyndman, H. M. *Further Reminiscences*, Macmillan, 1912.

134 Mann, T. *Tom Mann's Memoirs*, MacGibbon & Kee, 1923.

135 Snell, H. (Lord Snell). *Men, Movements, and Myself*, Dent, 1936.

136 Snowden, P. *An Autobiography*, Nicholson & Watson, 1934, 2 vols.

137 Webb, B. *My Apprenticeship*, Longmans, 1926.

Secondary reading

138 Pelling, H. *The Origins of the Labour Party*, 2nd edn, Oxford University Press, 1965: an invaluable introduction with an extensive bibliography.

140

139 Lynd, H. M. *England in the Eighteen-Eighties*, Oxford University Press, 1945.

140 Thompson, P. *Socialists, Liberals and Labour. The struggle for London, 1885–1914*, Routledge & Kegan Paul, 1967.

141 McBriar, A. M. *Fabian Socialism and English Politics*, Cambridge University Press, 1962.

142 Kent, W. *John Burns: Labour's lost leader*, Williams & Norgate, 1950.

143 Stewart, W. *J. Keir Hardie*, Cassell, 1921.

144 Hamilton, M. A. *Arthur Henderson*, Heinemann, 1938.

145 Tsuzuki, C. *H. M. Hyndman and British Socialism*, Oxford University Press, 1961.

146 Elton, G. (Lord Elton). *The Life of James Ramsay MacDonald*, Collins, 1939.

147 Torr, D. *Tom Mann and his Times*, vol. 1 (1856–1900), Lawrence & Wishart, 1956.

148 Cross, C. *Philip Snowden*, Barrie & Rockliff, 1966.

FICTION

149 Disraeli, B. *Sybil, or the Two Nations*, 1845; Oxford University Press, 1926.

150 Gaskell, E. *Mary Barton*, 1847; Dent, Everyman, 1964.

151 Kingsley, C. *Alton Locke*, 1850; Cassell paperback, 1967.

152 Eliot, G. *Felix Holt, the Radical*, 1866; Panther, 1965.

153 Osborne, J. *A Subject for Scandal and Concern*, Faber, 1961: a television play about G. J. Holyoake's trial and imprisonment, freely adapted from Holyoake's own account (**114**).

BIOGRAPHICAL REFERENCE BOOKS

154 Wheeler, J. M. *A Biographical Dictionary of Freethinkers of all Ages and Nations*, Progressive Publishing Co., 1889.

155 Boase, F. *Modern English Biography, containing Many Thousand Concise Memoirs of Persons who have died during the years 1851–1900*, Truro, Netherton & Worth, 1890–1921, 3 vols and 3 vols of supplements.

156 McCabe, J. *A Biographical Dictionary of Modern Rationalists*, Watts, 1920.

Index

Index

Index

145

151

Index

Walsh, William, 84
War Fly Sheet, 60
Ward, 'Zion', 9
Warner Street Temperance Hall, 55
Washington, George, 23
Watson, James, 31, 35, 36, 37, 39, 40,
    44, 49, 51, 53, 57, 58, 61, (80)
Watts, Charles, 56, 57, 58
Watts, Charles Albert, 58
Watts, John, 56
weavers, 26, 27, 36
Webb, Mrs Beatrice, 85, (137)
Webb, Sidney, 74, (24)
Wellington, Duke of, 27
Wesley, John, 10
West Ham, 76
West London Ethical Society, 83
West Riding Secular Alliance, 54
Whigs, 19, 27, 44, 78
Whitty, the Reverend, J. F., 5
Wigan, 33
Wilberforce, William, 29, 41

Wilkes, John, 19, 27; 'Wilkes and
    Liberty', 63
Williams, Thomas, 22, 25
Wisbech, 33
Wollstonecraft, Mary, 23
women's rights, 59, 65
Wooler, Jonathan, *Black Dwarf*, 28, 29,
    30, 31
Woolston, Thomas, 17, 18; *Six Dis-
    courses on the Miracles of Our Saviour*, 18
working classes (see also Labour), 3, 4,
    11, 12, 13, 14, 21, 22, 26, 27, 28, 40,
    42, 59, 60, 65, 66, 73, 76, 79, 81, 84,
    86, 87, **doc. 5**, (17)
World War I, 86

Yorkshire, 13, 26, 39, 54, 55, 65, 75
Yorkshire Factory Times, 75
Yorkshire Tribune, 54, 64–5

Zetetic Societies, 33